Instant Pot Cookbook: 80 Delicious Recipes to Make in a Pressure Cooker

By

Stephanie N. Collins

Legal & Disclaimer

The information contained in this book is not designed to replace or take the place of any form of medicine or professional medical advice. The information in this book has been provided for educational and entertainment purposes only.

The information contained in this book has been compiled from sources deemed reliable, and it is accurate to the best of the Author's knowledge; however, the Author cannot guarantee its accuracy and validity and cannot be held liable for any errors or omissions. Changes are periodically made to this book. You must consult your doctor or get professional medical advice before using any of the suggested remedies, techniques, or information in this book.

Upon using the information contained in this book, you agree to hold harmless the Author from and against any damages, costs, and expenses, including any legal fees potentially resulting from the application of any of the information provided by this guide. This disclaimer applies to any damages or injury caused by the use and application, whether directly or indirectly, of any advice or information presented, whether for breach of contract, tort, negligence, personal injury, criminal intent, or under any other cause of action.

Nutrition information should be considered an estimate only. Different nutrition calculators give you different results.

You agree to accept all risks of using the information presented inside this book. You need to consult a professional medical practitioner in order to ensure you are both able and healthy enough to participate in this program.

Table of Contents

Introduction

For a second, think about these next few questions carefully:

Are you always busy and never get enough time to cook the dishes that you really want? Do you want to cook nutritious and flavorful meals without having the need to "babysit" and watch it carefully like it is a life or death situation? Do you want to cook various types of dishes just by using one simple cooking appliance?

Then, your questions have been answered! The Instant Pot is the revolutionary answer to all of those questions. It is programmable, and it's one gadget that does the work of seven different cooking appliances. You can sauté or brown the meats and vegetables in it. You can use it as a slow cooker, pressure cooker, food warmer, rice cooker, stockpot, and even as a yogurt maker.

If you are someone who's extremely busy every day in your life, then, you will be happy to discover the marvelous blessings of pressure cooking. Why? Because pressure cooking is a way of cooking that not only saves energy, it also saves a lot of time – by slashing the number of hours to minutes.

Now, you might be thinking, "How does a pressure cooker achieve this?" Simple! A pressure cooker is a cooking vessel that is well-sealed. When water is heated up inside a well-sealed container, pressure builds up inside the container.

When this pressure rises, it raises the cooking temperature, which cooks your meals much faster.

Now that you've got an idea about the marvels of pressure cooking, let us begin a new and exciting journey in your kitchen with instant pot recipes!

Chapter 1: Step-by-Step Instant Pot Cooking and Smart Tips

Parts and Design of the Instant Pot

Before we get into the step-by-step tips on how to use your instant pot, you must become familiar with the parts of your cooking equipment.

The Housing

The housing holds the inner pot. This is where the sensors, heating element, and the control box is located. The control box is the heart of the pot. It monitors and regulates the pressure and temperature of the pot. When you press a function key, the control box is what controls the cooking cycles, heating, and time.

The Lid Lock

The lid of the pot contains the gasket and the sealing ring. When you close and lock the lid, the pot will become an airtight chamber and helps build up the pressure when the pot is heated. If you don't close the lid of your pot properly, it will not switch on for cooking.

The Inner Pot

This is the removable part of the cooking pot. It's made from high quality aluminum or stainless steel. It is dishwasher-friendly and the sizes range from 5.3-10.5 UK pints or 3-6 liters. The inner pot is where the ingredients are placed for cooking.

Safety Valves

The Instant Pot has two safety valves. There's the pressure valve and the float valve with a safety pin. Some models come with a safety pin that prevents a user from accidentally opening the pot while there is still pressure inside the pot. When there is a lot of pressure, the float valve pushes itself up and locks the lid from opening, preventing any accidental openings.

The pressure release regulator valve is designed to prevent steam from escaping while cooking and it is what releases the pressure when the cooking cycle is finished. In a conventional pressure cooker, excessive pressure will push the valve. In an instant pot, an electronic failure will cause the valve to release pressure.

Step-by-Step Instant Pot Cooking and Smart Tips

Now that you are familiar with the parts of an instant pot, follow the steps and tips below for a sure way to cook delicious dishes. Although the instant pot is an intelligent cooker that cooks food with high pressure ranging from 10.15 to 11 psi or cooking temperatures of 239F to 244F or 115C to

118C, there are basic cooking steps, safety measures, and tips to ensure that you are cooking food properly.

Open the Lid

Hold the lid handle, rotate it 30 degrees counterclockwise until the downward and the upward triangle with "OPEN" are aligned.

Check the Anti-Block Shield, Sealing Ring, and Float Valve

- The sealing ring should be well seated on the sealing ring rack – you will be able to turn it counterclockwise and clockwise with little effort when it is seated properly.
- The anti-block shield must be properly mounted on the steam release pipe.
- You should be able to easily move the float valve up and down.

Place the Ingredients in the Inner Pot

You can put the ingredients in the inner pot while it's in the housing or you can take it out before putting the ingredients in.

- When cooking beans, dried vegetables, and rice, do not fill the inner pot ½ full.
- Do not fill the inner pot more than ⅔ full.

Return Inner Pot to the Housing

If you took out the inner pot from the housing or just washed it, then make sure that you remove any foreign objects and wipe it dry. Make sure that there are no foreign objects on the heating element in the housing.

- After putting the inner pot in the housing, rotate it slightly to make sure that there is contact with the heating element.

Close and Lock the Lid

Hold the lid handle, rotate it 30 degrees clockwise until the downward and the upward triangle with "CLOSE" are aligned.

Close the Steam Valve

If you are pressure cooking in your instant pot, make sure that the steam handle is turned to "SEALING."

Connect the Cord and Plug your Pot to the Electrical Outlet

The LED display will show "OFF", ready for you to select a function key.

Select the Function Key that You Need

You can press any of the function keys - keep warm, yogurt, slow cook, steaming, bean and chili, meat and stew, poultry, soup, sauté/browning, congee/porridge, multigrain rice, and rice. When a function key is pressed, the indicator will light up. If you need to press another function, do it within 10 seconds after pressing a function key.

Set the Timer

You can change the cooking time by pressing the "+" or "-"
keys to add or lessen the cooking time. The cooking will start
after 10 seconds.

- The instant will beep and the led will display ON to
  indicate that it is heating up – this will take about 10 to
  15 minutes, depending on whether you are cooking
  fresh or frozen, the kind of food you are cooking, and
  the amount.
- It's normal to see traces of steam while the instant pot
  is heating and building up pressure. When the ideal
  pressure is reached, the float valve pop up and the led
  display will change from ON to the pre-set time of the
  function key or the time you programmed – it will count
  down to the end of the cooking cycle.
- It's also normal to see steam or smoke and sputtering
  while the cooking cycle is in process. The low clicking
  sounds you hear is also normal, so don't worry – this is
  the heating element switching from off to on to regulate
  the pressure.
- If you want to cancel the cooking process, press the
  WARM/CANCEL key.
- When the cooking cycle is finished and the food is
  cooked, the pot will automatically switch to KEEP
  WARM and the led display will show "L0:02 which will
  count up to 10 hours. When the 10 hours of keep warm
  mode is up, the pot will automatically switch to standby
  mode.

Release the Pressure

Press the "KEEP WARM/CANCEL" key to stop the cooking cycle and then release the pressure.

- Quick Release

   Turn the steam release handle to VENTING and wait for the float valve to go down - this means all the pressure from the pot is released. When quick releasing the pressure, make sure that the steam hole is away from you or any surface that can be damaged by hot steam. Use and oven mitt, heat-resistant silicone gloves, or a long-handles spoon so your hands are safe from the hot steam.

- Natural Release

   Just let the pressure come down naturally while the pot is in the keep warm mode for about 10-15 minutes or until the float valve goes down.

Open the Lid

Hold the lid handle, rotate it 30 degrees counterclockwise until the downward and the upward triangle with "OPEN" are aligned.

- Vacuum can suck the lid. If this happens, turn the steam release handle to VENTING to let the air in into the pot when you open the lid.

- If the float valve is stuck due to food debris and stickiness, use a pen or a chopstick to push it down – only do this when you are sure the pressure is released.

How Do I Convert My Favorite Recipes for Instant Pot Cooking?

It will not always be a direct conversion, so it's best to stick for recipes that are suitable for pressure cooking. You can convert stovetop pressure cooker recipes for instant pot cooking – just increase the cooking time to about 15 to 20 percent. Increase the time to 11-12 minutes for 10 minutes stovetop cooking time, 23-24 minutes for 20 minutes, and 34-36 minutes for 30 minutes, so on.

Instant Pot Smart Tips

Here are a few tips to ensure that your first instant pot cooking is hassle-free and safe.

- Place the instant pot far from a heated gas, electric, or oven burner.
- Place the pot in a stable, secure surface or location.
- Always plug the pot in the recommended 60Hz or 10-120V.

- Check the pressure release devices, especially if you have been using the pot for quite some time since food debris and particles can clog the steam release valve.
- Make sure that there is at least 1 cup water in the pot if you are pressure cooking dishes, particularly if you are steaming food.
- Do not let the cords touch any hot surface or hang over the edge of the counter where it can be disturbed and dislodged.
- Do not touch hot surfaces of the instant pot because they can burn.
- Always release the pressure before opening the lid of the pot.

Turn the pot off before you unplug and make sure the heated parts are completely cool before taking them off for cleaning.

The instant pot is one tool for sautéing, simmering, pressure cooking, slow cooking, steaming, boiling, canning, and last but not the least, to make yogurt.

Just dump all the ingredients in it, cover with its lid, select one of the pre-built cooking options, then adjust the timer and pressure cooking setting and leave the rest of the work to the instant pot.

The instant pot promotes efficient, automated, hassle-free, and time-saving cooking for any meal. Yes, its star feature of being a multi-purpose kitchen utensil makes it perfect to make any meal. From a healthy breakfast to a scrumptious snack, mouthwatering dinners to heavenly desserts, any meal can be conveniently put together in it. The instant pot is one tool for sautéing, simmering, pressure cooking, slow cooking, steaming, boiling, canning, and last but not the least, to make yogurt.

Just dump all the ingredients in it, cover with its lid, select one of the pre-built cooking options, then adjust the timer and pressure cooking setting and leave the rest of the work to the instant pot.

Are you ready to start your instant pot cooking journey? Then check the recipes.

Chapter 2: Breakfast

Pancake

Yield: 1 pancake

Time taken: 50 minutes

Ingredients

- 2 cups all-purpose flour
- 2 tablespoons white sugar
- 2½ teaspoons baking powder
- 2 eggs
- 1½ cups milk, unsweetened

Directions

1. Grease inside the instant pot with coconut oil spray.
2. Take a large bowl and beat together eggs and milk until combined using an electric mixer.
3. Mix in remaining ingredients until batter is smooth.
4. Spoon the batter into the instant pot and smooth top with a spatula.
5. Plug in the instant pot, close the lid, and make sure pressure indicator is positioned to its right place.
6. Select the "Manual" option and adjust cooking time to 40 minutes.
7. Then choose the low-pressure cooking setting and let cook.
8. The cooking timer will start once the pressure builds, about 10 to 12 minutes.
9. Upon beeping of the timer, press "Cancel" and select the "Keep warm" option, or unplug the instant pot, and do quick pressure release.
10. When the pressure is released completely, uncover the instant pot, and insert toothpick to check if the pancake is cooked through and the top is nicely golden brown and crispy.

11. Continue cooking for few more minutes at low pressure if the pancake is uncooked.
12. Use a spatula to remove pancake from pot.
13. Serve with melted butter and heated maple syrup or your favorite topping.

Nutrition Facts

Per serving | Calories: 1341 | Total Fat: 22.84g | Saturated Fat: 9.973g | Cholesterol: 364mg | Sodium: 304mg | Potassium: 2159mg | Carbohydrates: 232.81g | Fiber: 7g | Sugars: 37.34g | Protein: 48.44g | Vitamin A: 46% | Vitamin C: 0% | Calcium: 106% | Iron: 80%

Lemon Blueberry Breakfast Cake

Yield: 2 cakes

Time taken: 60 minutes

Ingredients

- 2 cups fresh blueberries
- 2 cups all-purpose flour
- ½ teaspoon salt
- ¾ cup white sugar
- ½ cup powdered sugar
- 2 teaspoons baking powder
- ½ cup unsalted butter, softened
- 1 teaspoon vanilla extract
- 1 lemon, zested
- Half of a lemon, juiced
- 1 egg
- ½ cup buttermilk
- ⅔ cup water

Directions

1. Take a round baking dish, big enough to fit into the instant pot, grease and flour; set aside until required.
2. In a medium-sized bowl, place flour and stir in salt and baking powder until mixed.

24

3. Reserve 2 tablespoons of flour mixture for tossing with the blueberries.
4. In a separate large bowl, stir in sugar, lemon zest, and butter using an electric mixture until combined.
5. Then mix in vanilla and egg until incorporated.
6. Stir in flour mixture, 2 to 3 tablespoons at a time, until incorporated.
7. Lightly toss the blueberries with reserved flour and gently fold into batter.
8. Spoon half of this mixture into prepared baking dish and smooth the top using a spatula.
9. Plug in the instant pot, pour in water, and insert a trivet stand or steamer basket.
10. Make a sling with aluminum foil to remove the baking dish and place baking dish on the trivet or basket.
11. Close the instant pot lid and make sure pressure indicator is positioned to its right place.
12. Select the "Manual" option and adjust cooking time to 30minutes.
13. Then choose the high-pressure cooking setting and let cook.
14. The cooking timer will start once the pressure builds, about 10 to 12 minutes.
15. Upon beeping of the timer, press "Cancel" and select the "Keep warm" option, or unplug the instant pot, and do quick pressure release.
16. When the pressure is released completely, uncover the instant pot, use a sling to lift out the baking dish, and let rest for 5 minutes.
17. Repeat with remaining batter.

18. Meanwhile, stir together lemon juice and powdered sugar.
19. Drizzle this syrup over cake and slice to serve.

Nutrition Facts

Per serving | Calories: 1300 | Total Fat: 35.26g | Saturated Fat: 20.5g | Cholesterol: 144mg | Sodium: 783mg | Potassium: 1046mg | Carbohydrates: 229.71g | Fiber: 7.4g | Sugars: 123.28g | Protein: 20.84g | Vitamin A: 51% | Vitamin C: 31% | Calcium: 44% | Iron: 46%

Twice Baked Potatoes Casserole

Yield: 10 servings

Time taken: 35 minutes

Ingredients

- 4 slices of bacon, cooked and crumbled
- 5 pounds of potatoes
- ½ cup chopped green onions, and more for top
- 1½ teaspoons salt or to taste
- ¾ teaspoon ground black pepper or to taste
- 2 tablespoons ranch seasoning mix
- 6 ounces of unsalted butter
- 2 cups shredded Cheddar cheese, and more for top
- 1 cup sour cream
- 1 cup water
- 8 fluid ounces milk, unsweetened

Directions

1. Rinse potatoes and then cut into bite-size pieces. Don't peel the potatoes.
2. Plug in the instant pot, add potatoes with water, then close the lid and make sure pressure indicator is positioned to its right place.
3. Select the "Manual" option and adjust cooking time to 6minutes.

4. Then choose the high-pressure cooking setting and let cook.
5. The cooking timer will start once the pressure builds, about 10 to 12 minutes.
6. Upon beeping of the timer, press "Cancel" and select the "Keep warm" option, or unplug the instant pot, and do quick pressure release.
7. Meanwhile, set the oven to 350°F and let preheat. When the pressure is released completely, uncover the instant pot, and stir in butter and milk. Using a potato masher, mash the potatoes.
8. Stir in ranch seasoning mix and sour cream until mixed well.
9. Fold in cheese and green onion and spoon this dish in a square baking dish, lightly greased with non-stick cooking oil.
10. Smooth the top using a spatula and then evenly top with more green onions and cheese.
11. Place baking dish in the oven and let bake for 20 minutes or until top is nicely golden brown.
12. Serve straightaway.

Nutrition Facts

Per serving | Calories: 461 | Total Fat: 25.54g | Saturated Fat: 12.838g | Cholesterol: 55mg | Sodium: 756mg | Potassium: 1158mg | Carbohydrates: 44.23g | Fiber: 5.3g | Sugars: 3.6g | Protein: 14.74g | Vitamin A: 37% | Vitamin C: 61% | Calcium: 29% | Iron: 12%

Hard Boiled Eggs

Yield: 6 eggs

Time taken: 20 minutes

Ingredients

- 6 eggs, chilled
- 1 cup cold water

Directions

1. In an instant pot, pour water and then insert a trivet stand or a steamer basket.
2. Place eggs in the steamer basket, then plug in the instant pot and close with its lid. Make sure pressure indicator is positioned to its right place.
3. Select the "Manual" option and then press adjust to set cooking time to 8 minutes.
4. Then press "Pressure" button to select the high-pressure cooking setting and let cook.
5. The cooking timer will start once the pressure builds, which will take 10 to 12 minutes.
6. Upon beeping of the timer, press "Cancel/Keep warm" option, or unplug the instant pot, and do quick pressure release.
7. When the pressure is released completely, uncover the instant pot and carefully remove the eggs and submerge them in a cold-water bath for 5 minutes.
8. Peel the shell of the eggs and serve straightaway.

Nutrition Facts

Per serving | Calories: 63 | Total Fat: 4.18g | Saturated Fat: 1.375g | Cholesterol: 164mg | Sodium: 63mg | Potassium: 61mg | Carbohydrates: 0.32g | Fiber: 0g | Sugars: 0.16g | Protein: 5.53g | Vitamin A: 10% | Vitamin C: 0% | Calcium: 3% | Iron: 4%

Burrito Casserole

Yield: 6 burritos

Time taken: 25 minutes

Ingredients

- 6 ounces ham steak, cubed
- 2 pounds red potatoes, peeled and cubed
- 1 medium-sized avocado, peeled, cored and sliced
- ¼ cup chopped white onion
- 1 jalapeno pepper, diced
- ½ teaspoon salt
- ¾ teaspoon taco seasoning
- ½ cup tomato salsa
- 1 cup and 1 tablespoon water, divided
- 4 eggs
- Marinated onions as needed
- 6 coconut flour tortillas, warmed

Directions

1. Place eggs in a baking dish, big enough to fit into the instant pot.
2. Using an electric mixer, beat in salt, red chili, taco seasoning, and 1 tablespoon water until combined.
3. Then stir in ham pieces, jalapeno, white onion, and potatoes until mixed.

4. Plug in the instant pot, pour in water, and insert a trivet stand or steamer basket.
5. Cover baking dish with aluminum foil and place on the trivet or basket.
6. Close the instant pot lid and make sure pressure indicator is positioned to its right place.
7. Select the "Manual" option and adjust cooking time to 13 minutes.
8. Then choose the high-pressure cooking setting and let cook.
9. The cooking timer will start once the pressure builds, about 10 to 12 minutes.
10. Upon beeping of the timer, press "Cancel" and select the "Keep warm" option, or unplug the instant pot, and let pressure release naturally.
11. Meanwhile, warm tortillas in a medium-sized skillet pan, about 30 seconds on each side.
12. When the pressure is released completely, uncover the instant pot and carefully remove the baking dish.
13. Evenly fill each burrito with egg mixture, top with salsa, avocado slices, and marinated onions.
14. Fold to wrap burritos and serve straightaway.

Nutrition Facts

Per serving | Calories: 313 | Total Fat: 10.06g | Saturated Fat: 2.236g | Cholesterol: 122mg | Sodium: 837mg | Potassium: 1127mg | Carbohydrates: 43.07g | Fiber: 7g | Sugars: 4.44g | Protein: 14.88g | Vitamin A: 16% | Vitamin C: 40% | Calcium: 10% | Iron: 15%

Banana French Toasts

Yield: 6 toasts

Time taken: 35 minutes

Ingredients

- 4 medium-sized bananas, peeled and sliced
- 4 tablespoons pecans, chopped
- 6 slices of French bread
- 1 tablespoon white sugar
- 2 tablespoons brown sugar
- ½ teaspoon ground cinnamon
- 1 teaspoon vanilla extract
- 3 eggs, slightly beaten
- 2 tablespoons grated chilled butter, and more as needed for greasing
- ¼ cup cream cheese
- ½ cup milk
- ¾ cup water
- Pure maple syrup as needed for serving

Directions

1. Take a round baking dish large enough to fit into the instant pot and grease it with butter.
2. Cut bread into cubes and arrange some of the bread cubes on the bottom of the greased baking dish.

33

3. Top with a layer of banana slices and then sprinkle with 1 tablespoon brown sugar.
4. Place cream cheese in a microwave ovenproof bowl and let microwave for 40 seconds or until melted completely.
5. Spread cream cheese evenly over the banana layer and then cover with remaining bread cubes and banana slices in separate layers.
6. Sprinkle with remaining 1 tablespoon of brown sugar and scatter with 2 tablespoons pecans and butter.
7. In a bowl, beat together eggs until frothy.
8. Then beat in white sugar, cinnamon, vanilla, and milk until combined.
9. Pour this mixture evenly into the baking dish and smooth the top with a spatula.
10. Plug in the instant pot, pour in water, and insert a trivet stand or steamer basket.
11. Make a sling with aluminum foil to remove the baking dish and place baking dish on the trivet or basket. You will simply need a nice grade of aluminum foil – you don't want cheap foil that breaks down with cooking or does not hold strong; use a brand name foil.
12. Close the instant pot lid and make sure pressure indicator is positioned to its right place.
13. Select the "Porridge" option and adjust cooking time to 5minutes.
14. Then choose the high-pressure cooking setting and let cook.
15. The cooking timer will start once the pressure builds, about 10 to 12 minutes.

16. Upon beeping of the timer, press "Cancel" and select the "Keep warm" option, or unplug the instant pot, and let pressure release naturally.
17. When the pressure is released completely, uncover the instant pot, use sling to lift out the baking dish.
18. Let rest for 5 minutes, then top with remaining pecans, drizzle with maple syrup, and serve.

Nutrition Facts

Per serving | Calories: 622 | Total Fat: 16.36g | Saturated Fat: 6.406g | Cholesterol: 103mg | Sodium: 954mg | Potassium: 549mg | Carbohydrates: 100.73g | Fiber: 5.7g | Sugars: 25.7g | Protein: 20.39g | Vitamin A: 18% | Vitamin C: 9% | Calcium: 14% | Iron: 35%

Crustless Meat Quiche

Yield: 4 servings

Time taken: 40 minutes

Ingredients

- 1 cup cooked ground sausage
- ½ cup diced ham
- 4 slices of bacon, cooked and crumbled
- 3 medium-sized green onions, chopped
- ¼ teaspoon salt
- ⅛ teaspoon ground black pepper
- 6 eggs, beaten
- 1 cup grated parmesan cheese and more as needed
- ½ cup milk, unsweetened
- 1 cup water

Directions

1. Plug in the instant pot, add water, insert a trivet stand or steamer basket, then press "Sauté" button and let preheat.
2. In a bowl, lightly whisk the eggs, milk, salt, and black pepper until combined.
3. Take a 1-quart quiche dish, stir together sausage, ham, bacon, onion, and cheese until well mixed.
4. Evenly pour egg mixture and stir until combined.

5. Cover dish with aluminum foil and place on the trivet or steamer basket.*
6. Close instant pot lid and make sure pressure indicator is positioned to its right place.
7. Select the "Manual" option and adjust cooking time to 30 minutes.
8. Then choose the high-pressure cooking setting and let cook.
9. The cooking timer will start once the pressure builds, about 10 to 12 minutes.
10. Upon beeping of the timer, press "Cancel" and select "Keep warm" option or unplug the instant pot.
11. Wait 10 minutes and then release pressure naturally.
12. Meanwhile, switch on the broiler and let preheat.
13. When the pressure is released completely, uncover the instant pot, and carefully lift out the quiche dish.
14. Uncover dish, sprinkle cheese on top, and place quiche in the broiler to bake for 3 to 5 minutes or until cheese melts completely and the top is nicely golden brown.
15. Serve warm.

Notes: You can make a sling with aluminum foil to place the baking dish on the trivet or basket and remove the baking dish from the instant pot.

Nutrition Facts

Per serving | Calories: 490 | Total Fat: 33.77g | Saturated Fat: 9.433g | Cholesterol: 350mg | Sodium: 1783mg | Potassium: 674mg | Carbohydrates: 13.69g | Fiber: 1g | Sugars: 5.18g |

Protein: 32.66g | Vitamin A: 119% | Vitamin C: 9% | Calcium: 38% | Iron: 25%

Peach and Cream Oatmeal

Yield: 4 bowls

Time taken: 25 minutes

Ingredients

- 1 medium-sized peach, cored and chopped
- 2 cups rolled oats
- 2 tablespoons flax meal
- ½ cup chopped almonds
- 1 teaspoon vanilla extract
- 4 tablespoons maple syrup
- 4 cups water

Directions

1. In an instant pot, place oats, peaches, vanilla, and water and stir until well mixed.
2. Plug in the instant pot, close the lid, and make sure pressure indicator is positioned to its right place.
3. Select the "Porridge" option and adjust cooking time to 3minutes.
4. Then choose the high-pressure cooking setting and let cook.
5. The cooking timer will start once the pressure builds, about 10 to 12 minutes.

6. Upon beeping of the timer, press "Cancel" and select the "Keep warm" option, or unplug the instant pot, and let pressure release naturally.
7. When the pressure is released completely, uncover the instant pot, and evenly divide among four serving bowls.
8. Top with flax meal, almonds, maple syrup and serve.

Nutrition Facts

Per serving | Calories: 278 | Total Fat: 11.39g | Saturated Fat: 1.383g | Cholesterol: 0mg | Sodium: 10mg | Potassium: 487mg | Carbohydrates: 51.78g | Fiber: 9.8g | Sugars: 16.57g | Protein: 11.71g | Vitamin A: 5% | Vitamin C: 3% | Calcium: 15% | Iron: 21%

Bacon Ranch Potatoes

Yield: 6 servings

Time taken: 30 minutes

Ingredients

- 3 slices of bacon, chopped
- 2 pounds red potatoes
- 1 teaspoon salt
- 1 teaspoon garlic powder
- 2 teaspoons dried parsley
- $\frac{1}{3}$ cup Ranch dressing
- 2 tablespoons water*
- 4 ounces shredded cheddar cheese

Directions

1. Wash potatoes thoroughly and cut into 1-inch cubes.
2. Plug in the instant pot, add potatoes, bacon, and water and stir until well mixed.
3. Stir in salt, garlic powder, parsley, close the instant pot lid, and make sure pressure indicator is positioned to its right place.
4. Select the "Manual" option and adjust cooking time to 7 minutes.
5. Then choose the high-pressure cooking setting and let cook.

6. The cooking timer will start once the pressure builds, which will take 10 to 12 minutes.
7. Upon beeping of the timer, press "Cancel" and select "Keep warm" option, or unplug the instant pot, and let pressure release naturally.
8. When the pressure is released completely, uncover the instant pot, and stir in ranch dressing and cheese.
9. Serve straightaway.

*Note: This recipe was made with 6QT Instant Pot. If yours is bigger, then you may need to add 1-2 tablespoons of additional water and increase the cooking time by about 5-7 minutes.

Nutrition Facts

Per serving | Calories: 293 | Total Fat: 17.6g | Saturated Fat: 4.635g | Cholesterol: 23mg | Sodium: 717mg | Potassium: 785mg | Carbohydrates: 25.56g | Fiber: 2.6g | Sugars: 2.75g | Protein: 9.3g | Vitamin A: 10% | Vitamin C: 18% | Calcium: 15% | Iron: 7%

Apple Spice Steel Cut Oats

Yield: 2 servings

Time taken: 8 minutes

Ingredients

- 1 apple, medium-sized, peeled, then chopped into pieces
- ½ cup steel cut oats
- 1½ cups water
- 1 teaspoon ground cinnamon
- ¼ teaspoon allspice
- ⅛ teaspoon nutmeg
- Sweetener, your choice, to taste

Directions

1. Put the apple, oats, spices, and water in the instant pot.
2. Cover and lock the lid. Turn the steam valve to "Sealing ". Press the "Manual" key, set the pressure to "High", and set the timer for 3 minutes.
3. When the instant pot timer beeps, release the pressure naturally for 10-15 minutes or until the valve drops. Turn the steam valve to "Venting" to release the remaining pressure. Unlock and carefully open the lid.
4. Mix in your choice of sweetener.

5. Serve topped with your favorite nondairy milk or unsweetened vanilla.

Notes: If you don't like chewy oats, you can cook this dish longer.

Nutrition Facts

Per serving | Calories: 140 | Total Fat: 1.6g | Saturated Fat: 0g | Cholesterol: 0mg | Sodium: 8mg | Potassium: 203mg | Carbohydrates: 30.4g | Fiber: 5.5g | Sugars: 11.9g | Protein: 3.1g | Vitamin A: 0% | Vitamin C: 14% | Calcium: 3% | Iron: 8%

Buckwheat Porridge with Raisin and Banana

Yield: 3-4 servings

Time taken: 11 minutes

Ingredients

- 1 sliced banana
- 1 cup of raw buckwheat groats
- 1 teaspoon ground cinnamon
- ½ teaspoon vanilla
- ¼ cup raisins
- 3 cups rice milk
- Chopped nuts, optional

Directions

1. Rinse the buckwheat and put in the instant pot.
2. Add the banana, rice milk, vanilla, cinnamon, and raisins.
3. Cover and lock the lid. Turn the steam valve to "Sealing". Press the "Manual" key, set the pressure to "High", and set the timer for 6 minutes.
4. When the instant pot timer beeps, release the pressure naturally for 10-15 minutes or until the valve drops. Turn the steam valve to "Venting" to release remaining pressure. Unlock and carefully open the lid.

5. Stir the porridge to combine using a long-handles spoon.

6. Add more milk to individual servings, depending on preferred consistency. If desired, sprinkle with chopped nuts.

Nutrition Facts

Per serving | Calories: 329 | Total Fat: 3.4g | Saturated Fat: 0g | Cholesterol: 0mg | Sodium: 92mg | Potassium: 535mg | Carbohydrates: 72.3g | Fiber: 5.9g | Sugars: 13.1g | Protein: 6.3g | Vitamin A: 1% | Vitamin C: 8% | Calcium: 5% | Iron: 12%

Cheesy Ham and Egg Casserole

Yield: 5 servings

Time taken: 15 minutes (Preparation Time) + 3-4 hours (Cooking Time)

Ingredients

- 1 bag (32 ounces) frozen cubed hash browns
- 1 cup whole milk
- 1 onion, large-sized, diced
- 1 teaspoon pepper
- 1 teaspoon salt
- 10-12 large eggs
- 1-2 cups of chopped ham
- 2 cups of shredded cheddar cheese

Directions

1. Grease the instant pot inner pot with nonstick cooking spray. Spread ⅓ of the hash browns in the bottom of the pot. Top with ⅓ of the onions, ⅓ of the ham, and ⅓ of the cheese. Repeat the layers.
2. In a large-sized mixing bowl, beat the eggs with the milk, pepper, and salt until well mixed. Pour the egg mix over the potato and ham layers.
3. Cover and lock the lid. Turn the steam valve to "Sealing". Press the "Slow Cook" key, select the "Less" option, and set the timer for 3-4 hours.

Nutrition Facts

Per serving | Calories: 889 | Total Fat: 51.6g | Saturated Fat: 17.8g | Cholesterol: 440mg | Sodium: 1879mg | Potassium: 1408mg | Carbohydrates: 70.6g | Fiber: 6.7g | Sugars: 7.2g | Protein: 35.6g | Vitamin A: 20% | Vitamin C: 44% | Calcium: 47% | Iron: 20%

Creamy Coconut Steel-Cut Oats

Yield: 4 servings

Time taken: 7 minutes

Ingredients

- 1 cup steel cut oats
- 1 cup coconut milk, PLUS more for topping (I use full-fat canned coconut milk, but you can substitute with lighter varieties if desired)
- ½ cup of unsweetened coconut flakes
- 2 tablespoons of brown sugar
- 2 cups water
- 1 pinch salt
- 1 cinnamon stick OR ½ teaspoon ground cinnamon, optional

Directions

1. Put the coconut flakes in the instant pot. Press the "Sauté" key. Sauté the coconut flakes, frequently stirring, until starting to turn light brown – watch carefully to avoid burning. When the coconut flakes are light brown, set aside ½ for the topping.
2. Add the oats in the instant pot and cook for a couple of minutes more until the coconut flakes and the oats are fragrant.
3. Add the milk and the rest of the ingredients. Stir to mix.

4. Press the "Cancel" key to stop the sauté function. Cover and lock the lid. Turn the steam valve to "Sealing". Press the "Manual" key, set the pressure to "High", and set the timer for 2 minutes.
5. When the instant pot timer beeps, release the pressure naturally for 10 minutes. Turn the steam valve to "Venting" to release the remaining pressure. Unlock and carefully open the lid.
6. Serve warm, drizzled with coconut milk and 1 tablespoon of toasted coconut or with your desired toppings.

Nutrition Facts

Per serving | Calories: 269 | Total Fat: 19g | Saturated Fat: 15.9g | Cholesterol: 0mg | Sodium: 56mg | Potassium: 276mg | Carbohydrates: 23.3g | Fiber: 4.4g | Sugars: 7.2g | Protein: 4.4g | Vitamin A: 0% | Vitamin C: 4% | Calcium: 3% | Iron: 18%

Bacon and Blue Cheese Cauliflower

Yield: 8 servings

Time taken: 35 minutes

Ingredients

- 1 head (1½ pounds) cauliflower
- ½ pound bacon, thick-sliced variety, crumbled
- ⅓ cup 0% Greek Yogurt
- ⅓ cup ⅓-fat cream cheese, softened, optional,
- ⅓ cup mayonnaise (increase to ⅔ cup if omitting cream cheese)
- ¼ cup blue cheese, crumbled
- 4 sticks string cheese, cut into pieces

Directions

1. Trim the stems and the leaves off from the cauliflower head.
2. Set a trivet in the instant pot and pour in 1 cup of water. Put the whole cauliflower head on the trivet.
3. Cover and lock the lid. Turn the steam valve to "Sealing". Press the "Manual" key, set the pressure to "High", and set the timer for 0 (zero) minutes.
4. When the instant pot timer beeps, turn the steam valve to "Venting" to quick release the pressure. Unlock and carefully open the lid.

5. In a small-sized bowl, mix the mayonnaise with the cream cheese, yogurt, and ½ of the blue cheese crumbles. Spread the mayo mix over the surfaces of the cauliflower head, sprinkle with the bacon bits and the remaining ½ of the blue cheese.
6. Bake in a preheated 350F oven for 20 minutes.

Nutrition Facts

Per serving | Calories: 151 | Total Fat: 10,4g | Saturated Fat: 5g | Cholesterol: 26mg | Sodium: 273mg | Potassium: 306mg | Carbohydrates: 8g | Fiber: 2.1g | Sugars: 3.2g | Protein: 7.8g | Vitamin A: 5% | Vitamin C: 66% | Calcium: 17% | Iron: 3%

Pumpkin with Pecan Pie Granola Steel Cut Oats

Yield: 6 servings

Time taken: 15 minutes

Ingredients

- 1 cup pumpkin puree
- 1 cup steel-cut oats
- 1 tablespoon butter
- 1 teaspoon pumpkin pie spice
- ¼ cup maple syrup
- ¼ teaspoon salt
- 2 teaspoons cinnamon
- 3 cups water

Directions

1. Put the butter in the instant pot. Press "Sauté" and let the butter melt. Add the oats and toast, constantly stirring, for about 3 minutes or until they smell nutty.
2. Add the rest of the ingredients. Press the "Cancel" key to stop the sauté function. Cover and lock the lid. Turn the steam valve to "Sealing". Press the "Manual" key, set the pressure to "High", and set the timer for 10 minutes.
3. When the instant pot timer beeps, release the pressure naturally for 10 minutes. Turn the steam valve to

"Venting" to release remaining pressure. Unlock and carefully open the lid.

4. Stir the oats and remove the inner pot from the housing. Let the oats rest uncovered for about 5-10minutes or until thick to desired consistency.
5. Serve warm with the milk, pecan pie granola, and maple syrup, if desired.

Nutrition Facts

Per serving | Calories: 120 | Total Fat: 3g | Saturated Fat: 1.4g | Cholesterol: 5mg | Sodium: 118mg | Potassium: 167mg | Carbohydrates: 22.2g | Fiber: 3g | Sugars: 9.3g | Protein: 2.3g | Vitamin A: 128% | Vitamin C: 3% | Calcium: 4% | Iron: 8%

Orange Infused Steel Cut Oats

Yield: 6 servings

Time taken: 11 minutes

Ingredients

- 1 cup steel cut oats
- 1 tablespoon maple syrup
- ½ cup orange juice
- ½ teaspoon cinnamon
- ½ teaspoon vanilla extract
- 2 cups water
- 2 cups whole milk
- 2 tablespoons butter
- 2 tablespoons orange zest

Directions

1. Combine all the ingredients in an oven-safe glass bowl that will fit your instant pot until well mixed.
2. Pour 1 cup water into the instant pot and set a trivet in the pot.
3. Put the bowl on the trivet. Cover and lock the lid. Turn the steam valve to "Sealing". Press the "Manual" key, set the pressure to "High", and set the timer for 6 minutes.
4. When the instant pot timer beeps, release the pressure naturally for 10-15 minutes or until the valve drops.

Turn the steam valve to "Venting" to release remaining pressure. Unlock and carefully open the lid.

5. Stir the dried cranberries in the oat mix until well combined.

Nutrition Facts

Per serving | Calories: 156 | Total Fat: 7.4g | Saturated Fat: 4.1g | Cholesterol: 18mg | Sodium: 64mg | Potassium: 221mg | Carbohydrates: 18g | Fiber: 1.7g | Sugars: 8.2g | Protein: 4.6g | Vitamin A: 4% | Vitamin C: 33% | Calcium: 11% | Iron: 5%

Soy Yogurt

Yield: 4 servings

Time taken: 5 minutes (Preparation Time) + 14 hours (Cooking Time)

Ingredients

- 1 box (32 ounces) soy milk (use a brand with ONLY soybeans and water)
- 2 tablespoons plain vegan yogurt your choice

Directions

1. Divide the soy milk between 2 wide-mouth pint jars. Add 1 tablespoon yogurt into each jar and stir well.
2. Carefully put the jars in the instant pot – do not place a trivet in the pot. Cover and lock the lid. Turn the steam valve to "Sealing". Press the "Manual" key, set the pressure to "High", and set the timer for 14 hours.
3. When the instant pot timer beeps, turn the steam valve to "Venting" to quick release the pressure. Unlock and carefully open the lid.
4. Stir the yogurt and serve with your favorite yogurt toppings.

Notes: This yogurt can be kept in the fridge for about 5 days. Avoid cooking in the morning, otherwise your instant pot will be tied up all day and you won't be able to use the pot for anything else. Instead, start cooking your yogurt in the evening and it will be ready in the morning for breakfast.

Nutrition Facts

Per serving | Calories: 128 | Total Fat: 4.1g | Saturated Fat: 0.5g | Cholesterol: 0mg | Sodium: 121mg | Potassium: 286mg | Carbohydrates: 14.8g | Fiber: 1.4g | Sugars: 9.6g | Protein: 7.9g | Vitamin A: 0% | Vitamin C: 0% | Calcium: 7% | Iron: 8%

Cranberry Apple Steel Cut Oats

Yield: 6 servings

Time taken: 50 minutes

Ingredients

- 4 diced apples
- 3 cups water
- 2-4 tablespoons butter AND/OR virgin coconut oil
- 2 teaspoons vanilla, optional
- 2 cups steel cut oats
- 2 cups milk
- 1-2 teaspoons cinnamon
- ¼ cup maple syrup
- ½ teaspoon salt
- ½ teaspoon nutmeg
- 1 teaspoon fresh squeezed lemon juice
- 1 cup yogurt OR another cup milk OR part whey)
- 1½ cups fresh cranberries

Directions

1. Grease the bottom of the instant pot with butter AND/OR virgin coconut oil.
2. Except for the vanilla, salt, and maple syrup, put the rest of the ingredients in the pot and let soak overnight.

3. In the morning, add the maple syrup. Cover and lock the lid. Turn the steam valve to "Sealing". Press the "Porridge" key and let cook for 20 minutes preset time.
4. When the instant pot timer beeps, turn the steam valve to "Venting" to quick release the pressure. Unlock and carefully open the lid.
5. Stir in the milk and vanilla.

Notes: If you want to do less in the morning, you can add the milk, vanilla, and maple syrup to soak overnight.

Nutrition Facts

Per serving | Calories: 340 | Total Fat: 8.2g | Saturated Fat: 4.2g | Cholesterol: 19mg | Sodium: 296mg | Potassium: 481mg | Carbohydrates: 57.8g | Fiber: 7.6g | Sugars: 31.4g | Protein: 9.1g | Vitamin A: 4% | Vitamin C: 32% | Calcium: 21% | Iron: 12%

Breakfast Quinoa

Yield: 6 servings

Time taken: 6 minutes

Ingredients

- 1½ cups quinoa, uncooked, well rinsed
- ½ teaspoon vanilla
- ¼ teaspoon ground cinnamon
- 2¼ cups water
- 2 tablespoons maple syrup
- Pinch salt

Optional toppings:

- Fresh berries
- Milk
- Sliced almonds

Directions

1. Put all the ingredients into the instant pot.
2. Cover and lock the lid. Turn the steam valve to "Sealing". Press the "Manual" key, set the pressure to "High", and set the timer for 1 minute.
3. When the instant pot timer beeps, turn the steam valve to "Venting" to quick release the pressure. Unlock and carefully open the lid.

4. Fluff the quinoa and serve hot with milk, sliced almonds, and berries.

Nutrition Facts

Per serving | Calories: 340 | Total Fat: 8.2g | Saturated Fat: 0g | Cholesterol: 0mg | Sodium: 33mg | Potassium: 255mg | Carbohydrates: 31.9g | Fiber: 3g | Sugars: 4g | Protein: 6g | Vitamin A: 0% | Vitamin C: 0% | Calcium: 3% | Iron: 11%

Chapter 3: Lunch

Seafood Paella

Yield: 4 servings

Time taken: 55 minutes

Ingredients

- 1 cup seafood mix (squid, meaty white fish, scallops)
- 2 cups mixed shellfish (clams, mussels, shrimp)
- 2 cups rice, short-grain
- 1¾ cups vegetable stock or seafood stock
- 1 green bell pepper, diced

- 1 red bell pepper, diced
- 1 yellow onion, medium-sized, diced
- ⅛ teaspoon ground turmeric
- 2 teaspoons sea salt
- 4 tablespoons extra-virgin olive oil
- Large pinch saffron threads

Directions

1. Press the "Sauté" key of the instant pot. Put the olive oil in the pot and heat until the oil is hot. Add the peppers and onions. Sauté for about 4 minutes or until the onions are soft.
2. Stir in the rice, saffron, and seafood; sauté for 2 minutes. Add the stock, salt, and turmeric. Mix well. Arrange the shellfish on top of the rice mix – do not mix. Press the "Cancel" key to stop the sauté function. Cover and lock the lid. Turn the steam valve to "Sealing". Press the "Manual" key, set the pressure to "High", and set the timer for 6 minutes.
3. When the instant pot timer beeps, release the pressure naturally for 10-15 minutes or until the valve drops. Turn the steam valve to "Venting" to release the remaining pressure. Unlock and carefully open the lid.
4. Mix the paella well. Cover and let it stand for 1 minute before serving it.

Nutrition Facts

Per serving | Calories: 604 | Total Fat: 16.8g | Saturated Fat: 2.7g | Cholesterol: 112mg | Sodium: 1535mg | Potassium:

579mg | Carbohydrates: 86.6g | Fiber: 2.7g | Sugars: 5.6g | Protein: 25.3g | Vitamin A: 43% | Vitamin C: 202% | Calcium: 8% | Iron: 32%

Red Beans & Rice

Yield: 10 servings

Time taken: 1 hour

Ingredients

- 2 cups uncooked red kidney beans
- 10 cups cooked rice
- 1 pound chicken sausage, thinly sliced
- 1 medium-sized red bell pepper, seeded and diced
- 3 celery stalks, diced
- 1 medium-sized white onion, peeled and diced
- 1½ teaspoons minced garlic
- 1½ teaspoons salt or to taste
- ½ teaspoon ground black pepper
- ¼ teaspoon ground white pepper
- ½ teaspoon dried thyme
- 2 leaves bay
- 1 teaspoon hot sauce
- 7 cups water

Directions

1. Plug in the instant pot, add all the ingredients, except for chicken sausage and rice, and stir until well mixed.
2. Close the instant pot lid and make sure pressure indicator is positioned to its right place.

3. Select the "Manual" option and adjust cooking time to 28 minutes.
4. Then choose the high-pressure cooking setting and let cook.
5. The cooking timer will start once the pressure builds, about 10 to 12 minutes.
6. Upon beeping of the timer, press "Cancel" and select the "Keep warm" option, or unplug the instant pot, and do quick pressure release.
7. When the pressure is released completely, uncover the instant pot, and stir in chicken sausage.
8. Seal the instant pot lid again and switch it on.
9. Select the "Manual" option and adjust cooking time to 15 minutes.
10. Then choose the high-pressure cooking setting and let cook.
11. When the timer beeps, press "Cancel" and select the "Keep warm" option, or unplug the instant pot, and let pressure release naturally.
12. When the pressure is released completely, uncover the instant pot, remove bay leaves, and serve this mixture with boiled rice.

Nutrition Facts

Per serving | Calories: 392 | Total Fat: 7.13g | Saturated Fat: 2.361g | Cholesterol: 54mg | Sodium: 899mg | Potassium: 358mg | Carbohydrates: 66.66g | Fiber: 3.9g | Sugars: 2.85g | Protein: 13.6g | Vitamin A: 17% | Vitamin C: 23% | Calcium: 9% | Iron: 32%

Jacket Potato

Yield: 4 potatoes

Time taken: 20 minutes

Ingredients

- 4 medium-sized potatoes
- 2 teaspoons salt
- 2 teaspoons ground black pepper
- 1 tablespoon unsalted butter
- 6 fluid ounces water

Directions

1. Plug in the instant pot, pour water, and insert a trivet or a steamer basket.
2. Wash potatoes thoroughly, prick with fork, and season each with $\frac{1}{2}$ teaspoon or more of salt and black pepper.
3. Place potatoes on a steamer basket or trivet and close the lid. Make sure pressure indicator is positioned to its right place.
4. Select the "Steam" option and adjust cooking time to 20minutes.
5. Then choose the high-pressure cooking setting and let cook.
6. The cooking timer will start once the pressure builds, about 10 to 12 minutes.

7. Upon beeping of the timer, press "Cancel" and select the "Keep warm" option, or unplug the instant pot, and let pressure release naturally.
8. When the pressure is released completely, uncover the pot, carefully lift out potatoes, and serve straightaway.

Nutrition Facts

Per serving | Calories: 305 | Total Fat: 2.31g | Saturated Fat: 1.317g | Cholesterol: 4mg | Sodium: 1187mg | Potassium: 1575mg | Carbohydrates: 65.39g | Fiber: 8.15g | Sugars: 2.89g | Protein: 7.72g | Vitamin A: 3% | Vitamin C: 97% | Calcium: 6% | Iron: 17%

Butternut Cauliflower Soup

Yield: 6 cups

Time taken: 30 minutes

Ingredients

- 2 cups cubed butternut squash
- 1 pound cauliflower florets
- 1 medium-sized white onion, peeled and diced
- 1 cup chopped green onions
- 1½ teaspoons minced garlic
- ½ teaspoon salt
- ½ teaspoon red pepper flakes
- 1 teaspoon paprika
- 1 teaspoon dried thyme
- 6 tablespoons Sriracha sauce
- 2 teaspoons olive oil
- 2 cups vegetable broth
- ½ cup cream, unsweetened, or half and half
- 1½ cups grated Parmesan cheese

Directions

1. Plug in the instant pot, press "Sauté" option, add oil and let heat.
2. Add white onion and let cook for 3 minutes or until nicely golden brown, stirring occasionally.

3. Then stir in garlic and continue cooking for 1 minute or until fragrant.
4. Add butternut squash pieces, cauliflower florets, salt, red pepper flakes, paprika, thyme, and vegetable broth.
5. Stir until well mixed and close the lid. Make sure pressure indicator is positioned to its right place.
6. Select the "Manual" option and adjust cooking time to 5minutes.
7. Then choose the high-pressure cooking setting and let cook.
8. The cooking timer will start once the pressure builds, which will take 10 to 12 minutes.
9. Upon beeping of the timer, press "Cancel" and select the "Keep warm" option, or unplug the instant pot, and do quick pressure release.
10. When the pressure is released completely, uncover the instant pot and stir in cream.
11. Using an immersion blender, blend soup until smooth and then ladle into serving bowls.
12. Drizzle with a tablespoon of Sriracha sauce, green onion, and cheese, and serve.

Nutrition Facts

Per serving | Calories: 220 | Total Fat: 12.77g | Saturated Fat: 6.6g | Cholesterol: 35mg | Sodium: 991mg | Potassium: 572mg | Carbohydrates: 18.58g | Fiber: 3.5g | Sugars: 5.9g | Protein: 10.28g | Vitamin A: 271% | Vitamin C: 67% | Calcium: 29% | Iron: 6%

Wild Rice Pilaf

Yield: 3 cups

Time taken: 40 minutes

Ingredients

- 1 cup wild rice, rinsed and drained
- 1 cup brown rice, rinsed and drained
- ¼ cup chopped parsley
- 2 cups sliced mushrooms
- 1medium-sized onion, peeled and diced
- 1 teaspoon minced garlic
- 1 teaspoon salt or to taste
- ½ teaspoon ground black pepper or to taste
- 1⅔ tablespoons coconut oil
- 2½ teaspoons vegetable base
- 20 fluid ounces water

Directions

1. Plug in the instant pot, select "Sauté" option, add oil and let heat for 1 minute or until warm.
2. Then add onion and mushrooms and cook for 4 minutes or until onions are nicely golden brown, stirring frequently.
3. Stir in garlic and continue cooking for 30 seconds.

4. Add rice and cook for 2 to 3 minutes or until toasted, stirring constantly.
5. Then press "Cancel", pour in water, and stir in vegetable base thoroughly.
6. Scrape the bottom and sides of the pot to remove stuck rice.
7. Close the instant pot lid. Make sure pressure indicator is positioned to its right place.
8. Select the "Manual" option and adjust cooking time to 20minutes.
9. Then choose the high-pressure cooking setting and let cook.
10. The cooking timer will start once the pressure builds, about 10 to 12 minutes.
11. Upon beeping of the timer, press "Cancel" and select the "Keep warm" option, or unplug the instant pot, and let pressure release naturally.
12. When the pressure is released completely, uncover the instant pot, fluff rice with a fork, and stir in salt and black pepper to taste.
13. Garnish with parsley and serve straightaway.

Nutrition Facts

Per serving | Calories: 505 | Total Fat: 10.06g | Saturated Fat: 7.022g | Cholesterol: 0mg | Sodium: 793mg | Potassium: 474mg | Carbohydrates: 92.31g | Fiber: 6.5g | Sugars: 3.62g | Protein: 13.58g | Vitamin A: 34% | Vitamin C: 13% | Calcium: 7% | Iron: 14%

Hawaiian Fried Rice

Yield: 6 servings

Time taken: 40 minutes

Ingredients

- 1½ cups uncooked brown rice, rinsed
- 6 ounces cooked ham, cubed
- 1 cup chopped pineapple
- 1 red pepper, chopped
- chopped scallions for garnish (optional)
- 1 small white onion, peeled and diced
- 2 tablespoons soy sauce
- 3 eggs, beaten
- 1 tablespoon olive oil
- 2 cups water

Directions

1. Plug in the instant pot, press "Sauté" option, add oil and let heat.
2. Add white onion and red pepper, and let cook for 3 minutes or until onions are nicely golden brown, stirring occasionally.
3. Add ham and eggs and stir until mixed.
4. Let cook for 3 to 5 minutes or until cooked through.

5. Stir in rice, pineapple, soy sauce, and water, close the instant pot lid, and make sure pressure indicator is positioned to its right place.
6. Select the "Manual" option and adjust cooking time to 24 minutes.
7. Then choose the high-pressure cooking setting and let cook.
8. The cooking timer will start once the pressure builds, about 10 to 12 minutes.
9. Upon beeping of the timer, press "Cancel" and select the "Keep warm" option, or unplug the instant pot, and after 5 minutes, do quick pressure release.
10. When the pressure is released completely, uncover the instant pot, stir thoroughly, and divide evenly into serving bowls.
11. Garnish with scallion and serve.

Nutrition Facts

Per serving | Calories: 288 | Total Fat: 6.68g | Saturated Fat: 1.453g | Cholesterol: 93mg | Sodium: 570mg | Potassium: 412mg | Carbohydrates: 45.33g | Fiber: 2.4g | Sugars: 7.46g | Protein: 12.03g | Vitamin A: 10% | Vitamin C: 21% | Calcium: 5% | Iron: 10%

Chili-Lime Chicken

Yield: 6 servings

Time taken: 25 minutes

Ingredients

- 2 pounds boneless chicken breasts
- 3 teaspoons minced garlic
- 1 teaspoon onion powder
- 1 teaspoon salt
- ¼ teaspoon ground black pepper
- 1½ teaspoons red chili powder
- 1 teaspoon ground cumin
- ½ teaspoon liquid smoke
- 2 medium-sized limes, juiced

Directions

1. Rinse chicken breasts, cut in half, and add to the instant pot.
2. Add garlic, salt, black pepper, red chili powder, cumin, onion powder, liquid smoke, and lime juice.
3. Using hands covered with gloves, rubs chicken breasts with the seasonings thoroughly.
4. Close instant pot lid and make sure pressure indicator is positioned to its right place.
5. Select the "Manual" option and adjust cooking time to 6minutes.

6. Then choose the high-pressure cooking setting and let cook.
7. The cooking timer will start once the pressure builds, about 10 to 12 minutes.
8. Upon beeping of the timer, press "Cancel" and select the "Keep warm" option, or unplug the instant pot, and after 5 minutes do quick pressure release.
9. When the pressure is released completely, uncover the instant pot, and insert a food thermometer into chicken pieces.
10. The thermometer should read 165°F. If the proper temperature is not reached, cook two minutes more.
11. Transfer chicken pieces to a cutting board and shred using forks.
12. Return chicken to the instant pot and toss to coat with the cooking sauce.
13. Adjust seasoning and serve.

Nutrition Facts

Per serving | Calories: 193 | Total Fat: 4.16g | Saturated Fat: 0.877g | Cholesterol: 110mg | Sodium: 477mg | Potassium: 558mg | Carbohydrates: 2.69g | Fiber: 0.5g | Sugars: 0.44g | Protein: 34.4g | Vitamin A: 12% | Vitamin C: 13% | Calcium: 2% | Iron: 6%

Taco Ranch Chicken Chili

Yield: 4 servings

Time taken: 45 minutes

Ingredients

- 1.5 pounds chicken breasts, uncooked
- 3 (16 oz) cans white chili beans, do not drain
- Chopped cilantro for garnish (optional)
- 1 can (10 oz) tomatoes, I used Diced Tomatoes & Green Chilies
- 2½ tablespoons taco seasoning (1 packet)
- 1¼ tablespoons ranch seasoning mix (1 packet)
- 4 tablespoons sour cream

Directions

1. Plug in the instant pot, add chicken breast, beans with their liquid, tomatoes, taco seasoning, and ranch seasoning mix.
2. Stir until mixed, then close the lid and make sure pressure indicator is positioned to its right place.
3. Select the "Manual" option and adjust cooking time to 15 minutes.
4. Then choose the high-pressure cooking setting and let cook.
5. The cooking timer will start once the pressure builds, about 10 to 12 minutes.

6. Upon beeping of the timer, press "Cancel" and select the "Keep warm" option, or unplug the instant pot, and do quick pressure release.
7. When the pressure is released completely, uncover the instant pot. Carefully remove the chicken breasts, and use two forks to shred the chicken.
8. Return chicken to the pot and stir thoroughly.
9. Divide evenly among serving plates; top each plate with 1 tablespoon of sour cream and chopped cilantro.

Nutrition Facts

Per serving | Calories: 579 | Total Fat: 19g | Saturated Fat: 5.661g | Cholesterol: 113mg | Sodium: 1247mg | Potassium: 1142mg | Carbohydrates: 49.18g | Fiber: 13.4g | Sugars: 3.23g | Protein: 51.15g | Vitamin A: 30% | Vitamin C: 9% | Calcium: 18% | Iron: 27%

Jalapeno Pickles

Yield: 10 servings (1 tablespoon per serving)

Total Time Taken: 25 minutes

Ingredients

- 1 pound jalapeno peppers, sliced
- ¼ teaspoon garlic powder
- 1 teaspoon pickling salt
- 1½ teaspoons white sugar
- 1½ cups apple cider vinegar

Directions

1. In an instant pot, place all the ingredients and stir until mixed.
2. Plug in the instant pot, close the lid, and make sure pressure indicator is positioned to its right place.
3. Select pickle option on the instant pot setting pad or press "Manual" and adjust cooking time to 1 minute.
4. Then choose the high-pressure cooking setting and let cook.
5. The cooking timer will start once the pressure builds, which will take 10 to 12 minutes.
6. Upon beeping of the timer, press "Cancel" and select the "Keep warm" option, or unplug the instant pot, and let pressure release naturally.
7. Meanwhile, wash and sterilize pickle jars.

8. First, spoon peppers in the jar and then cover with cooking liquid. If cooking liquid isn't enough, then pour in the vinegar.
9. Seal jar tightly to store pickles or serve straightaway.

Nutrition Facts

Per serving | Calories: 24 | Total Fat: 0.17g | Saturated Fat: 0.042g | Cholesterol: 0mg | Sodium: 236mg | Potassium: 141mg | Carbohydrates: 4.02g | Fiber: 1.3g | Sugars: 2.68g | Protein: 0.43g | Vitamin A: 21% | Vitamin C: 72% | Calcium: 1% | Iron: 1%

Minestrone Soup

Yield: 6 servings

Time taken: 30 minutes

Ingredients

- 15 ounces cooked white beans
- 1 large carrot, peeled and diced
- ½ cup baby spinach leaves
- 2 stalks celery, diced
- 1 can (28 oz) whole peeled tomatoes, crushed
- 1 large white onion, peeled and diced
- 1½ teaspoons minced garlic
- 1 teaspoon salt (or to taste)
- ¾ teaspoon ground black pepper
- 1 teaspoon dried oregano
- 1 teaspoon dried basil
- 1 bay leaf
- 1 cup elbow pasta, uncooked
- 2 tablespoons olive oil
- 2–3 tablespoons green pesto
- 4 cups vegetable broth
- ⅓ cup grated parmesan cheese

Directions

1. Plug in the instant pot, press "Sauté" option, add oil and let heat.
2. Add carrot, celery, white onion, and garlic, and let cook for 3 minutes or until onions are nicely golden brown, stirring occasionally.
3. Then stir in spinach, crushed tomatoes, salt, black pepper, oregano, basil, and bay leaf.
4. Stir until well mixed then add elbow pasta and vegetable broth.
5. Close the instant pot lid and make sure pressure indicator is positioned to its right place.
6. Select the "Manual" option and adjust cooking time to 6 minutes.
7. Then choose the high-pressure cooking setting and let cook.
8. The cooking timer will start once the pressure builds, which will take 10 to 12 minutes.
9. Upon beeping of the timer, press "Cancel" and select the "Keep warm" option, or unplug the instant pot, and after 2 minutes do quick pressure release.
10. When the pressure is released completely, uncover the instant pot and stir in white beans.
11. Ladle soup into serving bowl; garnish each bowl with a tablespoon of pesto and parmesan cheese.
12. Serve warm.

Nutrition Facts

Per serving | Calories: 331 | Total Fat: 10.27g | Saturated Fat: 2.19g | Cholesterol: 33mg | Sodium: 968mg | Potassium:

662mg | Carbohydrates: 46.97g | Fiber: 7.1g | Sugars: 4.16g | Protein: 14.13g | Vitamin A: 123% | Vitamin C: 11% | Calcium: 16% | Iron: 26%

Potato Salad

Yield: 6 servings

Time taken: 30 minutes

Ingredients

- 2 pounds red potatoes, diced*
- ¼ cup sweet pickle relish
- ½ cup chopped parsley
- ¼ teaspoon garlic powder
- ¾ teaspoon salt
- ½ teaspoon ground black pepper or to taste
- 1 tablespoon honey
- ¼ cup Dijon mustard
- 2 tablespoons apple cider vinegar
- ½ cup mayonnaise
- 3 eggs
- 1 cup water

Directions

1. Plug in the instant pot, add water, and insert a trivet or steamer basket.
2. Place potatoes in the basket and then place eggs on top.

3. Close instant pot lid and make sure pressure indicator is positioned to its right place.
4. Select the "Manual" option and adjust cooking time to 5 minutes.
5. Then choose the high-pressure cooking setting and let cook.
6. The cooking timer will start once the pressure builds, about 10 to 12 minutes.
7. Meanwhile, place sweet pickle relish in a bowl and whisk in honey, mustard, vinegar, and mayonnaise until smooth.
8. Whisk in $\frac{1}{8}$ teaspoon each of salt and black pepper and set the dressing aside until required.
9. Upon beeping of the timer, press "Cancel" and select the "Keep warm" option, or unplug the instant pot, and do quick pressure release.
10. When the pressure is released completely, uncover the instant pot, and using tongs, transfer eggs in a chill water bath and let rest until cool.
11. Add potatoes into dressing bowl, with garlic powder and remaining salt and black pepper.
12. When the eggs are cool, peel them, dice into bite-size pieces, and add to the salad bowl.
13. Toss to combine.
14. Adjust seasoning, place salad in refrigerator until chilled and then serve.

*Notes: with red skinned potatoes, it's not necessary to remove the peel.

Nutrition Facts

Per serving | Calories: 214 | Total Fat: 6.33g | Saturated Fat: 1.395g | Cholesterol: 86mg | Sodium: 571mg | Potassium: 777mg | Carbohydrates: 34.88g | Fiber: 3.3g | Sugars: 8.83g | Protein: 6.31g | Vitamin A: 29% | Vitamin C: 26% | Calcium: 5% | Iron: 12%

Pork Shoulder Carnitas

Yield: 8 servings

Time taken: 50 minutes

Ingredients

- 4 pounds pork shoulder
- 2 cups of shredded iceberg lettuce
- 2 cups easy avocado salsa, recipe below
- 2 cups chicken stock, free range, organic
- $\frac{1}{4}$ teaspoon black pepper
- $\frac{1}{2}$ cup onion, rough chopped
- 1 teaspoon salt (I used Himalayan pink)
- 5 cloves garlic
- 8 whole tortillas, preferably cassava flour a.k.a. siete OR your preferred grain-free tortillas OR large-sized lettuce leaves

For the avocado salsa:

- 1 cup of diced avocado
- 1 pinch salt (I used Himalayan pink)
- 1 tablespoon jalapeno pepper
- 1 tablespoon lime juice, fresh squeezed
- 1 tablespoon red onion, minced
- $\frac{1}{2}$ cup cilantro, rough chopped, packed
- $\frac{1}{4}$ teaspoon black peppercorns, fresh ground

- ⅔ cup roma tomato, seeds removed and then diced (about 1 large-sized roma tomato)

Directions

1. Put the pork shoulder in the instant pot. Pour in the chicken stock/water. Add the onions and the garlic and then season the top of the pork with salt and pepper.
2. Cover and lock the lid. Turn the steam valve to "Sealing". Press the "Manual" key, set the pressure to "High", and set the timer for 45 minutes – cooking time will depend on the size of your pork shoulder. Cook longer, if needed, until the meat easily shreds when tested with a fork.
3. While the pork is cooking, put the tomato, cilantro, onion, and lime juice in a medium-sized mixing bowl. Stir to combine. Season with pepper, salt, and minced jalapeno pepper. Add the diced avocado and stir to combine. Set aside in the fridge until ready to use.
4. When the instant pot timer beeps, turn the steam valve to "Venting" to quick release the pressure. Unlock and carefully open the lid. Shred the pork meat.
5. To make the tacos, warm the tortillas until pliable over medium heat. Put a layer of shredded lettuce on a tortilla, top with the carnitas, and then with the avocado salsa. Serve immediately.

Nutrition Facts

Per serving | Calories: 1537 | Total Fat: 106g | Saturated Fat: 37.4g | Cholesterol: 408mg | Sodium: 1342mg | Potassium:

1968mg | Carbohydrates: 31.4g | Fiber: 6.8g | Sugars: 3.4g | Protein: 110.5g | Vitamin A: 50% | Vitamin C: 45% | Calcium: 17% | Iron: 49%

Italian Sausage

Yield: 5-6 servings

Time taken: 3 hours and 20 minutes

Ingredients

- 1 package (5-6 links) Italian Sausage (mild or hot)
- 1 can (10.5 ounces) mushroom gravy
- 1 can (8 ounces) pizza sauce
- 1 cup bell peppers, sliced
- Sausage rolls

Directions

1. Press the "Sauté" key of the instant pot. Add a bit of oil in the pot. Add Italian sausage and cook until all sides are browned.
2. When the sausages are browned, add the gravy, pizza sauce, and pepper slices into the pot. Stir to combine.
3. Cover and lock the lid. Turn the steam valve to "Sealing". Press the "Slow Cook" key and set the timer for 3 hours.
4. When the instant pot timer beeps, turn the steam valve to "Venting" to quick release the pressure. Unlock and carefully open the lid.
5. Serve on sausage rolls topped with some of the sauce and pepper slices.

Nutrition Facts

Per serving | Calories: 403 | Total Fat: 10.7g | Saturated Fat: 3.4g | Cholesterol: 13mg | Sodium: 3889mg | Potassium: 279mg | Carbohydrates: 62.9g | Fiber: 2g | Sugars: 5.4g | Protein: 15.4g | Vitamin A: 17% | Vitamin C: 91% | Calcium: 17% | Iron: 17%

French Dip Sandwiches

Yield: 8 servings

Time taken: 40 minutes

Ingredients

- 4 pounds beef roast
- ¾ cup soy sauce
- 1 teaspoon beef bouillon granules
- 2 teaspoons black peppercorns
- 1 tablespoon rosemary, dried
- 1 teaspoon cloves garlic, minced
- 8 hamburger buns

Directions

1. Cut off as much fat as you can from the roast and put the meat in the instant pot.
2. In a mixing bowl, mix the soy sauce with the peppercorns, bouillon, garlic, and rosemary. Pour the mix over the roast in the pot.
3. Pour water in the pot just enough to cover the roast. Cover and lock the lid. Turn the steam valve to "Sealing". Press the "Manual" key, set the pressure to "High", and set the timer for 35 minutes.
4. When the instant pot timer beeps, turn the steam valve to "Venting" to quick release the pressure. Unlock and carefully open the lid.

5. Shred the roast using 2 forks and serve on buns.

Nutrition Facts

Per serving | Calories: 515 | Total Fat: 15.4g | Saturated Fat: 5.7g | Cholesterol: 203mg | Sodium: 1635mg | Potassium: 1004mg | Carbohydrates: 16.4g | Fiber: 1.1g | Sugars: 2.2g | Protein: 73.1g | Vitamin A: 0% | Vitamin C: 1% | Calcium: 5% | Iron: 246%

Chorizo and Jalapeno Mac and Cheese

Yield: 2 servings

Time taken: 24 minutes

Ingredients

- 100 grams (about 3.5 ounces) chorizo sausage, sliced into thin discs
- 1 teaspoon mustard powder
- 100 grams (about 3.5 ounces or about ⅓ cup + 1⅓ tablespoons) evaporated milk
- 120 grams (about ¼ pound) macaroni pasta, dried
- 2 tablespoons jalapeno pepper, finely chopped, less or more to taste
- 20 grams (0.7 ounces) Parmesan, grated
- 2-3 spring onions, minced finely
- 250 ml (about 1 cup + 1 tablespoon or about 8.5 fl.oz.) water
- 50 grams (about 1.8 ounces) Double Gloucester or Red Leicester cheese
- 50 grams (about 1.8 ounces) mozzarella, grated
- Good grating of nutmeg (about 20 scratches on your plane or grater will do)

Directions

1. Press the "Sauté" key of the instant pot. Add the chorizo. Cook the chorizo for a couple of minutes,

frequently stirring, until the chorizo release their oil and no pearly while fat remaining. If there is a lot of oil, spoon away the excess, leaving about 1 tablespoon in the pot.

2. Press the "Cancel" key to stop the sauté function. Add the macaroni, nutmeg, mustard, and water. Stir to mix.
3. Cover and lock the lid. Turn the steam valve to "Sealing". Press the "Manual" key, set the pressure to "High", and set the timer for 4 minutes.
4. When the instant pot timer beeps, turn the steam valve to "Venting" to quick release the pressure. Unlock and carefully open the lid. There should be no or little excess water left and the macaroni is fully cooked. Press the "Cancel" key to stop the keep warm mode.
5. Stir in cheeses in the pot and continue stirring for about 30 seconds until no clumps remain.
6. Add the jalapeno peppers, evaporated milk, and spring onions. Stir to combine.

Nutrition Facts

Per serving | Calories: 597 | Total Fat: 26.9g | Saturated Fat: 9.5g | Cholesterol: 67mg | Sodium: 573mg | Potassium: 502mg | Carbohydrates: 53g | Fiber: 2.9g | Sugars: 7.6g | Protein: 34.5g | Vitamin A: 8% | Vitamin C: 11% | Calcium: 27% | Iron: 18%

Chicken Tortilla Soup

Yield: 4 servings

Time taken: 30 minutes

Ingredients

For the soup:

- 3 chicken breasts (about 12-16 ounces total)
- 1 can (15 ounces) black beans OR equivalent amount cooked beans
- 2 pieces (6-inch) corn tortillas, chopped into 1-inch squares
- 1 cup frozen corn
- 2 teaspoons chili powder
- 2 tablespoons fresh cilantro, chopped
- 2 cloves garlic, minced
- ¼ teaspoon ground cayenne pepper
- 1 teaspoon ground cumin
- 1 tablespoon olive oil
- 1 ripe tomato, very large-sized, chopped
- 1 onion, medium-sized, chopped
- 1 bay leaf
- 3-4 cups chicken broth OR 3-4 cups water plus 1 tablespoon 'Better Than Bouillon'

To serve:

- Canola OR your preferred oil, for frying
- Corn tortillas, sliced into strips
- Fresh cilantro
- Fresh squeezed lime juice
- Grated cheese

Directions

1. Press the "Sauté" key of the instant pot. Put the olive oil in the pot and add the onion; cook, frequently stirring, until soft. Add the garlic, tortilla squares, and cilantro. Stir to combine and cook for 1 minute. Add the black beans, tomato, chicken breasts, corn, 3 cups broth, and spices.
2. Press the "Cancel" key to stop the sauté function. Cover and lock the lid. Turn the steam valve to "Sealing". Press the "Soup" key and set the timer for 4 minutes.
3. While the soup is cooking, prepare the toppings for serving. Put oil in a medium-sized skillet and heat over medium heat until it is hot. Fry the tortilla chips until both sides are golden brown. Transfer the cooked tortilla chips on a plate lined with paper towel to drain excess oil. Lightly salt the tortillas immediately after they are cooked.
4. Wash and chop the cilantro, grate the cheese, and slice the lime into wedges.
5. When the instant pot timer beeps, turn the steam valve to "Venting" to quick release the pressure. Unlock and carefully open the lid.

6. Transfer the chicken into a plate and shred using 2 forks. Return the shredded chicken into the pot and stir to combine.
7. Ladle the soup into bowls. Garnish each serving with the cheese, cilantro, and a squeeze of lime juice, and then top with crisp tortillas.

Nutrition Facts

Per serving | Calories: 632 | Total Fat: 9.8g | Saturated Fat: 2.1g | Cholesterol: 65mg | Sodium: 659mg | Potassium: 2140mg | Carbohydrates: 84.4g | Fiber: 19.4g | Sugars: 5.8g | Protein: 54g | Vitamin A: 13% | Vitamin C: 13% | Calcium: 18% | Iron: 47%

Beef Stew

Yield: 8 servings

Time taken: 1 hour and 15 minutes

Ingredients

- 2½ pounds chuck roast, cut into bite sized pieces
- 1 pound carrots, cut into bite sized pieces
- 1 pound potatoes, cut into bite sized pieces
- 1 teaspoon kosher salt
- 1 teaspoon smoked paprika
- ½ teaspoon garlic powder
- 16 ounces chicken stock
- 16 ounces tomato sauce
- 2 onions, large-sized, cut into bite sized pieces
- 2-3 tablespoons vegetable oil

Directions

1. Press the "Sauté" key of the instant pot. Put the vegetable oil in the pot and heat. Cook the chuck roast in the pot until browned, sprinkling the meat with salt while cooking.
2. When the roast cubes are browned, add the tomato sauce, chicken stock, and smoked paprika.
3. Press the "Cancel" key to stop the sauté function. Cover and lock the lid. Turn the steam valve to

"Sealing". Press the "Manual" key, set the pressure to "High", and set the timer for 15 minutes.

4. When the instant pot timer beeps, turn the steam valve to "Venting" to quick release the pressure. Unlock and carefully open the lid. Add the vegetables in the pot.

5. Cover and lock the lid. Turn the steam valve to "Sealing". Press the "Manual" key, set the pressure to "High", and set the timer for another 30 minutes.

6. When the instant pot timer beeps, quick turn the steam valve to "Venting" to quick release the pressure. Unlock and carefully open the lid. Serve.

Nutrition Facts

Per serving | Calories: 427 | Total Fat: 15.5g | Saturated Fat: 5g | Cholesterol: 143mg | Sodium: 903mg | Potassium: 1061mg | Carbohydrates: 20.6g | Fiber: 4.3g | Sugars: 7.2g | Protein: 49.5g | Vitamin A: 196% | Vitamin C: 34% | Calcium: 5% | Iron: 36%

Sloppy Joes and Tangy Slaw

Yield: 6-8 servings

Time taken: 35 minutes

Ingredients

For the sloppy joes:

- 1 pound ground beef, extra lean, frozen or fresh
- 1 carrot, grated
- 1 cup chopped tomatoes, fresh or canned with its juices
- ½ cup (about 1.6 ounces) rolled oats
- 1½ teaspoons salt
- 1 cup water
- 1 red onion, medium-sized, chopped
- 1 red or green bell pepper, mediums-sized, chopped
- 1 tablespoon olive oil
- 1 tablespoon Worcestershire Sauce – optional
- 2 teaspoons garlic powder
- 4 tablespoons (about 2.8 ounces) tomato paste
- 4 tablespoons apple cider vinegar

For the tangy coleslaw:

- 2 tablespoons apple cider vinegar
- 2 carrots, grated (about 1 cup)
- ½ red onion, finely chopped

- ½ head cabbage, cut into quarters and then thinly sliced (about 5 cups)
- 1 tablespoon honey
- 1 tablespoon Dijon mustard, grainy variety

Directions

1. Press the "Sauté" key of the instant pot and wait until hot. Add the slab of frozen beef and cook for about 8 minutes each side or until browned. Push the beef to one side of the pot. Add the onions, carrots, and peppers in the cleared area. Sprinkle with the salt and garlic powder. Sauté for about 5 minutes or until the vegetables are soft.
2. Add the Worcestershire sauce, tomato paste, chopped tomatoes, water, and vinegar. Mix until well combined.
3. If the frozen meat is soft, break it into chunks and scrape any browned bits that stuck on the bottom of the pot. Bring to a boil. Add the oats – do not stir. Press the "Cancel" key to stop the sauté function. Cover and lock the lid. Turn the steam valve to "Sealing". Press the "Manual" key, set the pressure to "High", and set the timer for 10 minutes.
4. When the instant pot timer beeps, release the pressure in short bursts. Unlock and carefully open the lid.
5. Press the "Sauté" key. Cook for 5 minutes, constantly stirring, until the cooking liquid is reduced. Press the "Cancel" key to stop the sauté function and turn off the pot. Let stand for 5 minutes to thicken. Serve with coleslaw.

6. In a large-sized bowl, whisk the mustard, honey, and vinegar until well combined. Mix in the carrots, cabbage, and onions.

Nutrition Facts

Per serving | Calories: 266 | Total Fat: 7.8g | Saturated Fat: 2.2g | Cholesterol: 68mg | Sodium: 736mg | Potassium: 812mg | Carbohydrates: 22.7g | Fiber: 4.8g | Sugars: 11.4g | Protein: 26.3g | Vitamin A: 125% | Vitamin C: 118% | Calcium: 6% | Iron: 86%

Pork Barbecue Pulled Sandwiches

Yield: 8 servings

Time taken: 1 hour and 10 minutes

Ingredients

- 2½-3 pounds pork shoulder or roast, boneless, fat trimmed off
- 3 tablespoons brown sugar
- 2 tablespoons chili powder
- 2 tablespoons paprika
- 1 teaspoon cumin
- 1 teaspoon sea salt
- ½ teaspoon black pepper
- ¾ cup apple cider
- ½ cup barbecue sauce
- ¼ cup buffalo wing hot sauce
- 8 sandwich rolls or hamburger buns

Directions

1. Slicing against the grain, cut the pork into halves. Set aside.
2. In a small-sized bowl, combine the brown sugar with pepper, salt, cumin, paprika, and chili powder. Rub all the sides of the pork roast with the seasoning mix.

3. Put the barbecue sauce, buffalo sauce, and apple cider into the bottom of the instant pot. Stir to combine. Put the pork on top of the sauce mix. Cover and lock the lid. Turn the steam valve to "Sealing". Press the "Manual" key, set the pressure to "High", and set the timer for 45 minutes.
4. When the instant pot timer beeps, turn the steam valve to "Venting" to quick release the pressure. Unlock and carefully open the lid. Press the "Cancel" key to stop the keep warm mode.
5. Transfer the pork into a cutting board. Shred the meat using two forks – discard any excess fat.
6. Return the pork into the pot and mix with the sauce.
7. Serve on sandwiches or on top of hamburger buns with your favorite toppings.

Nutrition Facts

Per serving | Calories: 594 | Total Fat: 32.9g | Saturated Fat: 11.7g | Cholesterol: 128mg | Sodium: 923mg | Potassium: 665mg | Carbohydrates: 35.3g | Fiber: 2.4g | Sugars: 13g | Protein: 37.7g | Vitamin A: 31% | Vitamin C: 15% | Calcium: 11% | Iron: 24%

Chicken Chile Verde Taco and Avocado

Yield: 4-6 servings

Time taken: 55 minutes

Ingredients

- 3 pounds chicken breasts, skinless and boneless
- ½ tablespoon paprika, smoked or fancy
- ½ pound Anaheim peppers, stems and seeds removed, and cut into halves
- ½ cup water
- 1 yellow or white onion, quartered
- 1 tablespoon Kosher salt
- 1 tablespoon ground cumin
- 1 tablespoon fish sauce
- ¾ pound poblano peppers, stems and seeds removed, and cut into halves
- ¾ pound tomatillos OR 3-4 large-sized tomatillos, quartered, husks discarded
- 4-5 jalapeno peppers, stems and seeds removed, and cut into halves
- 4-6 garlic cloves, medium-sized, peeled

Directions

1. Put the chicken in the pot. Except for the fish sauce, add the rest of the ingredients in the instant pot. Stir to mix.
2. Cover and lock the lid. Turn the steam valve to "Sealing". Press the "Manual" key, set the pressure to "High", and set the timer for 25 minutes.
3. When the instant pot timer beeps, turn the steam valve to "Venting" to quickly release the pressure. Unlock and carefully open the lid.
4. Transfer the chicken into a plate. Pour the chili mixture into a blender. Add the fish sauce. Pulse for about 10 to 15 seconds or until desired consistency is achieved. Alternatively, you can add the fish sauce in the pot and use an immersion blender to puree.
5. Shred the chicken using two forks and return into the pot, along with the chili mix, if pureed in a blender. Keep warm.
6. Serve wrapped in tortillas with shredded cheese and sour cream or over rice or sweet rolls.

Nutrition Facts

Per serving | Calories: 739 | Total Fat: 27g | Saturated Fat: 7g | Cholesterol: 303mg | Sodium: 2764mg | Potassium: 1499mg | Carbohydrates: 18.9g | Fiber: 4.6g | Sugars: 6.3g | Protein: 102.3g | Vitamin A: 43% | Vitamin C: 370% | Calcium: 11% | Iron: 41%

Creamy Tomato Soup

Yield: 5 servings (1.5 cups per serving)

Time taken: 20 minutes

Ingredients

- 1 cup chicken broth
- 4 cans (14.5 oz each) organic diced tomatoes
- 1 tablespoon butter
- ½ cup heavy cream
- ½ onion, diced
- 2 tablespoons sugar
- 1 tablespoon dried basil
- Salt and pepper to taste
- Croutons or grated Parmesan for garnish (optional)

Directions

1. Plug in the instant pot, press "Sauté" option, add the butter and melt.
2. When the butter is completely melted, add the onions and sauté for 5-6 minutes or until soft.
3. Add the chicken broth, canned tomatoes (with liquid), sugar, and basil; stir to combine.
4. Press "Cancel" and close the instant pot lid, making sure pressure indicator is positioned to its right place.
5. Select the "Manual" option and adjust cooking time to 7 minutes.

6. Then choose the high-pressure cooking setting and let cook.
7. The cooking timer will start once the pressure builds, which will take 10 to 12 minutes.
8. Upon beeping of the timer, press "Cancel" and select "Keep warm" option, or unplug the instant pot, and let pressure release naturally.
9. When the pressure is released completely, uncover the instant pot, carefully transfer soup in a blender, and blend until smooth.
10. Pour blended soup back into the instant pot and stir in the heavy cream
11. Ladle soup into bowls; garnish with croutons or grated Parmesan.

Nutrition Facts

Per serving | Calories: 114 | Total Fat: 8.05g | Saturated Fat: 4.722g | Cholesterol: 25mg | Sodium: 381mg | Potassium: 280mg | Carbohydrates: 7.55g | Fiber: 1.8g | Sugars: 5.56g | Protein: 3.88g | Vitamin A: 28% | Vitamin C: 15% | Calcium: 6% | Iron: 4%

Marinated Beets

Yield: 4 servings

Time taken: 1 hour and 10 minutes

Ingredients

- 6 medium beets (about 2 inches in diameter)*
- 1 cup water
- 1 tablespoon olive oil
- 1 tablespoon apple cider vinegar
- 1 tablespoon lemon juice
- sea salt to taste
- black pepper to taste

Directions

1. Wash and trim the beets so the stems are about ½-inch and the roots about 2 inches or less.
2. Plug in the instant pot, pour in 1 cup of water, and insert a trivet stand or steamer basket.
3. Arrange beets in a single layer on the trivet or basket.
4. Cover and lock the lid. Turn the steam valve to "Sealing".
5. Press the "Manual" key, set the pressure to "High", and set the timer for 15 minutes.
6. When the instant pot timer beeps, turn the steam valve to "Venting" to quick release the pressure. Unlock and carefully open the lid.

7. Once the steam dissipates, poke a knife through a beet to check if it's cooked through. The beets should be firm but easy to poke. If they are not yet ready, cook them under high pressure for 2 to 5 more minutes.
8. Let beets cool till you can handle them safely.
9. Once the beets are cool, slice off the tops and slide the skins off**. Cut them into bite-size pieces and place in a large bowl.
10. Pour the vinegar, lemon juice, and olive oil over the beets and toss to coat; season with salt and pepper.
11. Allow to marinate for a half hour at room temperature.
12. Serve warm or chilled. They're great as a side dish, a snack, or even chopped up in salads.

*Notes: Cooking time will depend on the size of the beets.

**Notes: To avoid staining your fingers, wear rubber gloves when handling beets.

Nutrition Facts

Per serving | Calories: 64 | Total Fat: 3.52g | Cholesterol: 0mg | Sodium: 59mg | Potassium: 235mg | Carbohydrates: 7.77g | Fiber: 1.5g | Sugars: 6.08g | Protein: 1.27g | Vitamin A: 1% | Vitamin C: 6% | Calcium: 2% | Iron: 3%

Chapter 4: Dinner

Barbecue Ribs

Yield: 4 servings

Time taken: 28 minutes

Ingredients

- 1 rack (3 pounds) pork ribs
- 1 cup water
- 1 cup barbecue sauce

113

- Onion, garlic, and chipotle powder, to taste

Directions

1. Set a trivet in the bottom of the instant pot. Pour in 1 cup of water in the pot. Sprinkle the ribs with the onion powder, garlic powder, and chipotle powder. Coil the rib rack into a circle that will fit in your instant pot.
2. Cover and lock the lid. Turn the steam valve to "Sealing". Press the "Manual" key, set the pressure to "High", and set the timer for 25 minutes.
3. When the instant pot timer beeps, release the pressure naturally for 10-15 minutes or until the valve drops. Turn the steam valve to "Venting" to release the remaining pressure. Unlock and carefully open the lid.
4. Remove the rib from the pot and put in a baking sheet lined with foil. Coat the rib rack with the sauce. Broil for a couple of minutes or until the sauce is caramelized. Cut the ribs between the bones. Serve with more sauce.

Nutrition Facts

Per serving | Calories: 1023 | Total Fat: 60.4g | Saturated Fat: 21.4g | Cholesterol: 350mg | Sodium: 898mg | Potassium: 1110mg | Carbohydrates: 22.7g | Fiber: 0g | Sugars: 16.3g | Protein: 90.1g | Vitamin A: 3% | Vitamin C: 1% | Calcium: 12% | Iron: 26%

Cream of Asparagus Soup

Yield: 2 bowls

Time taken: 30 minutes

Ingredients:

- 2 ounces diced celery
- 18 ounces asparagus spears
- 4 ounces onion, finely chopped
- 1 teaspoon minced garlic
- 1½ tablespoons unsalted butter
- 1 teaspoon salt
- ½ cup cream
- 2 cups vegetable stock

Directions

1. Rinse asparagus, cut into 1½-inch pieces, and reserve the tips.
2. Plug in the instant pot, select "Sauté" option, add butter, and let melt completely.
3. Then add onions and let cook for 5 to 7 minutes or until softened, stirring frequently.
4. Add garlic and continue cooking for 60 seconds or until fragrant.
5. Add asparagus, pour in vegetable stock, and bring the mixture to a boil.

6. When the mixture comes to a boil, press "Cancel" and close the instant pot lid, making sure pressure indicator is positioned to its right place.
7. Select the "Manual" option and adjust cooking time to 5 minutes.
8. Then choose the high-pressure cooking setting and let cook.
9. The cooking timer will start once the pressure builds, which will take 10 to 12 minutes.
10. Upon beeping of the timer, press "Cancel" and select "Keep warm" option, or unplug the instant pot, and let pressure release naturally.
11. When the pressure is released completely, uncover the instant pot, and using an immersion blender, blend soup until smooth.
12. Pass the soup through a fine mesh sieve to get it ultra-smooth.
13. Plug in the instant pot, select "Sauté" option, and stir cream into the soup.
14. Let cook until warm.
15. Meanwhile, using a vegetable peeler, shave reserved asparagus tips.
16. Ladle soup into serving bowls, garnish with asparagus, and serve straightaway.

Nutrition Facts

Per serving | Calories: 257 | Total Fat: 17.78g | Saturated Fat: 10.931g | Cholesterol: 51mg | Sodium: 2163mg | Potassium: 743mg | Carbohydrates: 20.69g | Fiber: 6.4g | Sugars: 12.23g

| Protein: 8.32g | Vitamin A: 134% | Vitamin C: 25% | Calcium: 15% | Iron: 32%

Carnitas

Yield: 12 carnitas

Time taken: 1 hour and 20 minutes

Ingredients

- 3¼ pounds pork shoulder meat, boneless and trimmed
- 1 medium-sized white onion, peeled and chopped
- 2 teaspoons minced garlic
- 2 bay leaves
- 1 teaspoon salt or to taste
- ½ teaspoon ground black pepper
- 1 teaspoon ground cumin seed
- 1 teaspoon cinnamon powder
- 1 tablespoon soy sauce
- 2 tablespoons olive oil
- ¼ cup orange juice
- ⅘ cup chicken stock
- 12 corn tortillas
- Tomato salsa, as needed for serving
- 1 lime

Directions

1. Rinse pork meat and cut into 2-inch pieces.

2. Transfer pork pieces to an instant pot and add onion, garlic, bay leaves, salt, black pepper, ground cumin, cinnamon, soy sauce, and orange juice.
3. Stir well and let marinate for 20 minutes.
4. After 20 minutes, pour in the chicken stock and stir until just combined.
5. Plug in the instant pot, close the lid, and make sure pressure indicator is positioned to its right place.
6. Select the "Manual" option and adjust cooking time to 30 minutes.
7. Then choose the high-pressure cooking setting and let cook.
8. The cooking timer will start once the pressure builds, about 10 to 12 minutes.
9. Upon beeping of the timer, press "Cancel" and select the "Keep warm" option, or unplug the instant pot, and let pressure release naturally.
10. Meanwhile, switch on the broiler and let preheat to 450°F.
11. When the pressure is released completely, uncover the instant pot, and carefully transfer meat onto a baking tray.
12. Taste and adjust seasoning in the meat then drizzle with ¼ cup of the cooking liquid and oil.
13. Place the baking tray into the broiler and let broil for 10 minutes.
14. Then turn each piece of meat, drizzle with cooking liquid, and return baking tray to the oven.
15. Continue broiling until meat's surface is crispy.

119

16. Meanwhile, place a non-stick skillet over medium heat; warm tortilla in it.
17. Top pork pieces on warmed tortillas in equal portion and spoon with salsa. Squeeze the juice from lime over the pork. Serve.

Nutrition Facts

Per serving | Calories: 245 | Total Fat: 7.39g | Saturated Fat: 1.801g | Cholesterol: 74mg | Sodium: 394mg | Potassium: 570mg | Carbohydrates: 13.79g | Fiber: 1.9g | Sugars: 1.47g | Protein: 29.88g | Vitamin A: 1% | Vitamin C: 5% | Calcium: 4% | Iron: 9%

Pork Chops in Mushrooms Gravy

Yield: 4 servings

Time taken: 50 minutes

Ingredients

- 4 boneless pork loin chops (about 2 pounds)
- 8-9 large cremini mushrooms, stemmed and sliced
- 1 medium-sized white onion, minced
- 2 tablespoons minced garlic
- ⅛ teaspoon salt or to taste
- ⅛ teaspoon ground black pepper
- 2 tablespoons cornstarch
- 1 tablespoon soy sauce
- 1 tablespoon Worcestershire sauce
- 2 tablespoons peanut oil
- Dash of sherry wine
- 2 tablespoons water
- ¼ cup heavy cream
- 1 cup chicken stock, unsalted

Directions

1. Plug in the instant pot, select "Sauté" option, and let heat.
2. Pound pork evenly on both sides to the desired thickness – about a 1¼-inch thick.

121

3. Add 1 tablespoon oil to the pot then add pork pieces.
4. Cook each side for 2 minutes or until browned then transfer pork pieces to a plate.
5. Into the pot, add remaining 1 tablespoon oil then add mushrooms.
6. Let cook for 6 to 8 minutes or until liquid has almost evaporated.
7. Season with salt and black pepper and add onions and garlic.
8. Continue cooking for 2 minutes or until vegetables are soft.
9. Meanwhile, in a bowl, whisk together soy sauce, Worcestershire sauce, and chicken stock.
10. When the vegetables are soft, add wine into the pot and scrape the bottom of the pot to remove any browned bits.
11. Return pork pieces to the pot, pour in chicken stock mixture, and stir until mixed.
12. Close the instant pot lid and make sure pressure indicator is positioned to its right place.
13. Select the "Manual" option and adjust cooking time to 1 minute.
14. Then choose the high-pressure cooking setting and let cook.
15. The cooking timer will start once the pressure builds, which will take 10 to 12 minutes.
16. Upon beeping of the timer, press "Cancel" and select the "Keep warm" option, or unplug the instant pot, and let pressure release naturally.

17. When the pressure is released completely, uncover the instant pot, and remove pork pieces to a plate.
18. Plug in instant pot, press "Sauté" option, and stir in cream.
19. Stir together cornstarch and water and add to the pot, one-third portion at a time, until sauce reaches to desired thickness, adjusting the taste.
20. Evenly divide pork chops among serving platter, top with mushroom gravy, and serve immediately.

Nutrition Facts

Per serving | Calories: 446 | Total Fat: 18.22g | Saturated Fat: 5.841g | Cholesterol: 162mg | Sodium: 575mg | Potassium: 1198mg | Carbohydrates: 12.64g | Fiber: 1.1g | Sugars: 3.82g | Protein: 54.98g | Vitamin A: 5% | Vitamin C: 7% | Calcium: 4% | Iron: 11%

Chickpea, Sweet Potato and Spinach Curry

Yield: 2 servings

Time taken: 35 minutes

Ingredients

- 1½ cups sweet potato, peeled and chopped
- 2 cups chopped baby spinach
- 1 (15 oz) can chickpeas, drained
- 2 medium-sized tomatoes, chopped
- ¾ cup chopped red onion
- ½-inch ginger, chopped (optional)
- 1½ teaspoons minced garlic
- ¾ teaspoon salt or to taste
- ½ teaspoon red chili powder
- ¼ teaspoon ground black pepper
- ½ teaspoon ground turmeric
- ¼ teaspoon ground cinnamon
- ½ teaspoon garam masala or curry powder or Cajun spice mix
- 1 teaspoon coriander powder
- ½ teaspoon cumin seeds
- 1 teaspoon olive oil

- 1 teaspoon lemon juice
- 2 cups water

Directions

1. In a bowl, stir together red chili powder, black pepper, turmeric, cinnamon, garam masala, and coriander.
2. Plug in the instant pot, press the "Sauté" button, then add oil and let heat until warm. Add the cumin seeds; toast until they are fragrant, about 30 seconds.
3. Add onion, ginger, and garlic. Let cook for 2 minutes, stirring frequently.
4. Then add prepared spice mix, stir well, and continue to sauté for 30 seconds.
5. Add tomatoes and continue cooking for 3 minutes.
6. Press "Cancel" and add sweet potatoes and chickpeas.
7. Pour in water and stir in salt.
8. Close the instant pot lid and make sure pressure indicator is positioned to its right place.
9. Select the "Manual" option and adjust cooking time to 10 minutes.
10. Then choose the high-pressure cooking setting and let cook.
11. The cooking timer will start once the pressure builds, about 10 to 12 minutes.
12. Upon beeping of the timer, press "Cancel" and select the "Keep warm" option, or unplug the instant pot, and do quick pressure release.

13. When the pressure is released completely, uncover the instant pot. Taste and adjust with more salt and spice if needed.
14. Transfer curry to a serving plate. Serve with rice or quinoa.

Nutrition Facts

Per serving | Calories: 381 | Total Fat: 7.35g | Saturated Fat: 0.774g | Cholesterol: 0mg | Sodium: 1389mg | Potassium: 1468mg | Carbohydrates: 66.96g | Fiber: 18.9g | Sugars: 15.55g | Protein: 18.31g | Vitamin A: 1446% | Vitamin C: 46% | Calcium: 36% | Iron: 37%

Pasta Bolognese

Yield: 4 servings

Time taken: 30 minutes

Ingredients

- 16 ounces penne pasta, uncooked
- ½ pound ground beef
- 12 white mushrooms, sliced
- 1 celery, chopped
- 1 small white onion, peeled and sliced
- 1½ teaspoons minced garlic
- 1 teaspoon salt or to taste
- 1 teaspoon ground black pepper or to taste
- ⅛ teaspoon dried oregano
- ⅛ teaspoon dried basil
- 2 tablespoons soy sauce
- 1 tablespoon Worcestershire sauce
- 1 tablespoon fish sauce
- Dash of sherry wine
- 2 tablespoons olive oil
- 5.5 fluid ounces tomato paste
- ½ cup grated parmesan cheese
- 1 cup chicken stock
- 2 cups water

Directions

1. Plug in the instant pot, press "Sauté" button, and let heat until hot.
2. Add 1 tablespoon oil and then add ground beef with salt and black pepper.
3. Let cook for 5 minutes or until moisture evaporates completely and meat is nicely browned.
4. When done, transfer meat to a bowl and set aside until required.
5. Into the pot, add remaining 1 tablespoon oil and onion.
6. Season with $\frac{1}{8}$ teaspoon of salt and black pepper and let cook for 3 minutes or until onions are nicely golden brown.
7. Then stir in garlic and continue cooking for 30 seconds or until fragrant.
8. Add mushroom and celery and stir in oregano and basil.
9. Let cook for 1 minute and adjust seasoning.
10. Pour in sherry wine and scrape the bottom of the pan to remove any browned bits.
11. Return browned ground beef to the pot and stir in soy sauce, Worcestershire sauce, and fish sauce.
12. Pour in chicken stock and water and stir until well mixed.
13. Add pasta and top with tomato paste.
14. Adjust the seasoning and stir until pasta is well mixed into the sauce.
15. Close the instant pot lid and make sure pressure indicator is positioned to its right place.

16. Select the "Manual" option and adjust cooking time to 4 minutes.
17. Then choose the high-pressure cooking setting and let cook.
18. The cooking timer will start once the pressure builds, about 10 to 12 minutes.
19. Upon beeping of the timer, press "Cancel" and select the "Keep warm" option, or unplug the instant pot, and after 5 minutes, do quick pressure release.
20. When the pressure is released completely, uncover the instant pot and stir until combined.
21. Adjust the seasoning, and if the sauce is too thick, plug in instant pot, select "Sauté" option, and let cook until sauce reduces to desired thickness.
22. Garnish with cheese and serve immediately.

Nutrition Facts

Per serving | Calories: 468 | Total Fat: 22.46g | Saturated Fat: 7.065g | Cholesterol: 109mg | Sodium: 1940mg | Potassium: 652mg | Carbohydrates: 39g | Fiber: 4.7g | Sugars: 4.97g | Protein: 28.26g | Vitamin A: 18% | Vitamin C: 9% | Calcium: 18% | Iron: 26%

Teriyaki Rice with Chicken & Vegetables

Yield: 4 servings

Time taken: 45 minutes

Ingredients

- 1 cup long-grained rice, rinsed and drained
- 1 medium-sized boneless chicken breast, cubed
- ½ cup frozen shelled edamame beans, thawed
- 1 cup broccoli florets
- ½ cup chopped red bell peppers
- ½ cup shredded carrots
- ¼ cup chopped green onions, for garnish
- ½ teaspoon grated ginger
- 1 teaspoon minced garlic
- 1 teaspoon salt or to taste
- ½ teaspoon ground black pepper or to taste
- 2 teaspoons cornstarch
- ½ cup soy sauce
- ⅓ cup apple cider vinegar
- 2 tablespoons Mirin (or dry sherry)
- ⅓ cup honey
- 2 tablespoons olive oil
- 1¼ cups water and more as needed, divided
- Sesame seeds, for garnish

Directions

1. Plug in the instant pot, press "Sauté" button, and let heat until warm.
2. Meanwhile, whisk together cornstarch, soy sauce, apple cider vinegar, Mirin, and honey until combined.
3. Pour this mixture into the instant pot, gradually stir in ¼ cup water, and boil until sauce gets thick.
4. When done, pour sauce into a bowl and set aside until required.
5. Rinse the pot, wipe dry using kitchen towels, then add oil and let heat until hot.
6. Add chicken pieces and season with salt and black pepper.
7. Let cook for 3 minutes or until nicely golden brown on all sides.
8. Stir in ginger and garlic and continue cooking for 20 seconds or until fragrant.
9. Add edamame beans, broccoli florets, red bell pepper, carrots, rice, and 1 cup water along with ¾ portion of the prepared sauce.
10. Stir until just mixed and close the instant pot lid, making sure pressure indicator is positioned to its right place.
11. Select the "Manual" option and adjust cooking time to 5 minutes.
12. Then choose the high-pressure cooking setting and let cook.
13. The cooking timer will start once the pressure builds, about 10 to 12 minutes.

14. Upon beeping of the timer, press "Cancel" and select the "Keep warm" option, or unplug the instant pot, and do quick pressure release.
15. When the pressure is released completely, uncover the instant pot, and stir until combined.
16. Garnish with sesame seeds and green onion, drizzle with remaining prepared sauce, and serve immediately.

Nutrition Facts

Per serving | Calories: 479 | Total Fat: 12.18g | Saturated Fat: 1.89g | Cholesterol: 43mg | Sodium: 2656mg | Potassium: 690mg | Carbohydrates: 69.86g | Fiber: 5.2g | Sugars: 26.43g | Protein: 24.72g | Vitamin A: 147% | Vitamin C: 47% | Calcium: 7% | Iron: 17%

Chicken Congee

Yield: 7 cups

Time taken: 1 hour and 5 minutes

Ingredients

- ¾ cup Jasmine rice
- 6 chicken drumsticks
- Green onions as needed for garnish
- 1 tablespoon ginger, sliced into strips
- 2 teaspoons salt or to taste
- 6.5-7 cups water, chilled

Directions

1. Measure the rice and put it in the instant pot, then run cool water over the rice to cover. Rinse the rice in cold water, rubbing the grains of rice between your fingers. Pour out the used water and repeat this process until water is clear. Drain well.
2. Add chicken, ginger and pour in chilled water and stir until just mixed.
3. Plug in the instant pot, close the lid, and make sure pressure indicator is positioned to its right place.
4. Select the "Manual" option and adjust cooking time to 30 minutes.
5. Then choose the high-pressure cooking setting and let cook.

6. The cooking timer will start once the pressure builds, about 10 to 12 minutes.
7. Upon beeping of the timer, press "Cancel" and select "Keep warm" option, or unplug the instant pot, and let pressure release naturally.
8. When the pressure is released completely, uncover the instant pot, and stir until just mixed. The congee will look watery.
9. Plug in the instant pot, press the "Sauté" option, and let congee simmer for 10 to 15 minutes or until it reaches desired consistency, stirring occasionally.
10. When done, press "Cancel" and transfer chicken pieces to a cutting board.
11. Shred chicken pieces and discard bones and skin.
12. Return chicken pieces to the pot and stir until combined.
13. Garnish with green onions and serve.

Nutrition Facts

Per serving | Calories: 221 | Total Fat: 12.94g | Saturated Fat: 3.278g | Cholesterol: 103mg | Sodium: 794mg | Potassium: 432mg | Carbohydrates: 6.72g | Fiber: 2.7g | Sugars: 0.18g | Protein: 21.89g | Vitamin A: 3% | Vitamin C: 0% | Calcium: 4% | Iron: 18%

Whole Chicken and Veggies

Yield: 4 servings (1 serving per person)

Total Time Taken: 45 minutes

Ingredients

- 1 whole chicken (about 4 lbs)
- 2 large carrots
- 2 large sweet potatoes
- 1½ teaspoons salt or to taste
- ½ teaspoon ground black pepper or to taste
- 1 tablespoon chopped rosemary
- 1 tablespoon unsalted butter
- 1 cup chicken broth or water

Directions

1. Peel carrots and sweet potatoes, then break carrot in half and cut sweet potatoes into 2-inch cubes.
2. In an instant pot, pour chicken broth and then insert trivet stand or steamer basket.
3. Rinse chicken until clean, pat dry, and then season with salt and black pepper.
4. Place chicken on the basket, top with vegetables, and then sprinkle with rosemary and add butter.
5. Plug in the instant pot, close the lid and make sure pressure indicator is positioned to its right place.

6. Select the "Manual" option and adjust cooking time to 27 minutes.
7. Then choose the high-pressure cooking setting and let cook.
8. The cooking timer will start once the pressure builds, about 10 to 12 minutes.
9. Upon beeping of the timer, press "Cancel" and select the "Keep warm" option, or unplug the instant pot, and let pressure release naturally.
10. Meanwhile, switch on broiler in the oven and let preheat.
11. When the pressure is released completely, uncover the instant pot and transfer chicken to a baking sheet using tongs.
12. Place baking sheet under the broiler and let broil for 3 to 4 minutes or until chicken is nicely golden brown and crisp.
13. Serve chicken with vegetables straightaway.

Nutrition Facts

Per serving | Calories: 476 | Total Fat: 22.52g | Saturated Fat: 6.945g | Cholesterol: 135mg | Sodium: 1192mg | Potassium: 938mg | Carbohydrates: 22.64g | Fiber: 4.1g | Sugars: 7.67g | Protein: 43.94g | Vitamin A: 1013% | Vitamin C: 27% | Calcium: 8% | Iron: 16%

Pepper Steak

Yield: 6 to 8 servings

Time taken: 1 hour and 15 minutes

Ingredients

- 30 oz round steak, cut into thin strips
- 2 medium-sized green bell peppers, seeded and cut into strips
- 3 medium-sized white onions, peeled and thinly sliced
- 1 teaspoon salt
- ½ teaspoon ground black pepper
- 2 tablespoons molasses
- 2 tablespoons cornstarch
- 2 tablespoons olive oil
- Water as needed

Directions

1. Place a large non-stick skillet pan over medium heat, add oil, and let heat.
2. Add steak strips and let cook for 8 to 10 minutes or until nicely browned.
3. Add onion and continue cooking for 3 to 5 minutes or until softened.
4. Spoon this mixture into an instant pot and stir in salt, black pepper, and molasses.

137

5. Plug in the instant pot, cover steak with water, and cover the instant pot with its lid, making sure pressure indicator is positioned to its right place.
6. Select the "Meat/Stew" option and adjust cooking time to 30 minutes.
7. Then choose the high-pressure cooking setting and let cook.
8. The cooking timer will start once the pressure builds, about 10 to 12 minutes.
9. Upon beeping of the timer, press "Cancel" and select the "Keep warm" option, or unplug the instant pot, and let pressure release naturally.
10. When the pressure is released completely, uncover the instant pot, and stir in peppers.
11. Let cook for 7 to 10 minutes or until tender.
12. Meanwhile, stir together cornstarch and 3 tablespoons chilled water until combined.
13. When peppers are cooked through, add cornstarch mixture and stir well until sauce reaches desired thickness.
14. Serve with boiled rice.

Nutrition Facts

Per serving | Calories: 306 | Total Fat: 13.27g | Saturated Fat: 4.102g | Cholesterol: 106mg | Sodium: 385mg | Potassium: 405mg | Carbohydrates: 6.89g | Fiber: 0.2g | Sugars: 4.45g | Protein: 37.29g | Vitamin A: 0% | Vitamin C: 1% | Calcium: 2% | Iron: 19%

Cauliflower Curry

Yield: 3 servings (½ cup per serving)

Total Time Taken: 20 minutes

Ingredients

- 4 cups cauliflower florets
- 1 medium-sized potato, peeled and cut into small wedges
- 2 medium-sized tomatoes, diced
- 1 medium-sized white onion, peeled and sliced
- 1 teaspoon salt
- 1 tablespoon red chili powder
- 1½ teaspoons Indian garam masala powder*
- ½ teaspoon turmeric powder
- ½ tablespoon cumin seeds
- ½ tablespoon coriander powder
- ½ teaspoon cumin powder
- 1 tablespoon olive oil
- ¼ cup water
- ¼ cup chopped cilantro

Directions

1. Plug in the instant pot, select "Sauté" option, add oil, and let preheat.

139

2. Then add cumin seeds and sauté for 30 to 45 seconds or until fragrant.
3. Add onion and let cook for 2 to 3 minutes or until softened, stirring frequently.
4. Stir in tomatoes and continue cooking for 1 minute.
5. Stir in salt, red chili powder, garam masala powder, turmeric powder, coriander, and cumin.
6. Add cauliflower florets, potatoes, and water and stir until well mixed.
7. Press "Cancel" and close the lid. Make sure pressure indicator is positioned to its right place.
8. Select the "Manual" option and adjust cooking time to 3 minutes.
9. Then choose the high-pressure cooking setting and let cook.
10. The cooking timer will start once the pressure builds, about 10 to 12 minutes.
11. Upon beeping of the timer, press "Cancel" and select the "Keep warm" option, or unplug the instant pot, and let pressure release naturally.
12. Then uncover the instant pot, stir the curry gently, garnish with cilantro, and serve.

Notes: Add only ½ teaspoon to make your curry less spicy.

Nutrition Facts

Per serving | Calories: 331 | Total Fat: 5.84g | Saturated Fat: 0.946g | Cholesterol: 0mg | Sodium: 906mg | Potassium: 1019mg | Carbohydrates: 25.28g | Fiber: 6.7g | Sugars: 5.81g

| Protein: 5.61g | Vitamin A: 68% | Vitamin C: 126% | Calcium: 8% | Iron: 17%

Lemon Chicken Curry

Yield: 6 servings

Time taken: 40 minutes

Ingredients

- 32 oz chicken breasts
- 32 oz chicken thighs
- ½ teaspoon salt
- 1 teaspoon ground turmeric
- 1 tablespoon curry powder
- 1 teaspoon lemon zest
- ¼ cup lemon juice
- 1 can (13.5 fl.oz.) coconut milk, unsweetened

Directions

1. Separate cream from the coconut milk and pour milk in a large bowl.
2. Whisk in salt, turmeric, curry powder, and lemon juice until combined and then pour a little of this mixture in the instant pot.
3. Add chicken into the pot, pour in the rest of mixture, and top with coconut cream.
4. Plug in the instant pot, close the lid, and make sure pressure indicator is positioned to its right place.
5. Select the "Poultry" option and adjust cooking time to 15 minutes.

6. Then choose the high-pressure cooking setting and let cook.
7. The cooking timer will start once the pressure builds, which will take 10 to 12 minutes.
8. Upon beeping of the timer, press "Cancel" and select the "Keep warm" option, or unplug the instant pot, and do quick pressure release.
9. When the pressure is released completely, uncover the instant pot. Test chicken for doneness by cutting open one of the large pieces of chicken and ensuring the flesh has changed from pink to white.
10. If still pink, return the instant pot to high pressure cooking for 5 to 10 minutes.
11. When done, transfer chicken pieces to a cutting board and shred meat using forks.
12. Sprinkle lemon zest over the chicken.
13. Serve with cooked rice or steamed vegetables.

Nutrition Facts

Per serving | Calories: 757 | Total Fat: 55.38g | Saturated Fat: 25.162g | Cholesterol: 245mg | Sodium: 422mg | Potassium: 852mg | Carbohydrates: 5.79g | Fiber: 2.2g | Sugars: 2.57g | Protein: 58.29g | Vitamin A: 10% | Vitamin C: 8% | Calcium: 5% | Iron: 21%

Buffalo Chicken Meatballs

Yield: 18 to 24 meatballs

Time taken: 45 minutes

Ingredients

- 1.5 pounds ground chicken
- 2 green onions, peeled and thinly sliced and more for garnishing
- 1 teaspoon minced garlic
- 1 teaspoon sea salt
- ¾ cup almond meal
- 6 tablespoons hot sauce
- 2 tablespoons ghee plus extra to grease your hands
- 4 tablespoons butter, unsalted

Directions

1. Place ground chicken in a large bowl and add green onions, garlic, salt, and almond meal.
2. With hand, mix the ingredients until combined.
3. Grease hand with ghee and shape mixture into 1 to 2-inch meatballs.
4. Plug in the instant pot, press "Sauté" option, add butter, and let heat until butter melts completely.
5. Add meatballs in a single layer and let cook for 1 minute per side until nicely browned on all sides.

6. Meanwhile, in a microwave-safe bowl, stir together hot sauce and unsalted butter and let microwave for 1 minute or until butter melts completely, stirring every 20 seconds.
7. When the meatballs are browned, return them to the instant pot and evenly top with hot sauce mixture.
8. Close the instant pot lid and make sure pressure indicator is positioned to its right place.
9. Select the "Poultry" option and adjust cooking time to 20 minutes.
10. Then choose the high-pressure cooking setting and let cook.
11. The cooking timer will start once the pressure builds, about 10 to 12 minutes.
12. Upon beeping of the timer, press "Cancel" and select the "Keep warm" option, or unplug the instant pot, and do quick pressure release.
13. When the pressure is released completely, uncover the instant pot, and serve straightaway with cooked rice.

Nutrition Facts

Per serving | Calories: 96 | Total Fat: 7.63g | Saturated Fat: 2.962g | Cholesterol: 37mg | Sodium: 265mg | Potassium: 203mg | Carbohydrates: 0.93g | Fiber: 0.5g | Sugars: 0.25g | Protein: 6.44g | Vitamin A: 7% | Vitamin C: 4% | Calcium: 1% | Iron: 2%

Cheeseburger Meatloaf and Mashed Potatoes

Yield: 6 servings

Time taken: 45 minutes

Ingredients

- 1½ pounds ground beef
- 1 cup bread crumbs
- 1 cup water
- 1 tablespoon Oregano
- 1 teaspoon garlic powder
- 1 teaspoon onion powder
- ¼ cup milk
- 2½ pounds potatoes, diced
- 2 eggs
- 2 tablespoons butter
- 3 tablespoons milk
- 4 ounces cheddar cheese
- 4 ounces pepper jack cheese
- 4 ounces shredded cheddar

Directions

1. Put the diced potatoes in the instant pot and add 1 cup of water.

2. In a mixing bowl, mix the ground beef with the 3 tablespoons milk, breadcrumbs, eggs, and seasonings. Add 4 ounces of shredded cheddar and mix. Put the beef mix into a wax paper and spread out. Cut the pepper jack and cheddar cheese into lengthwise pieces and put in the center of the beef mixture. Roll the meat so the cheeses are in the center of the roll. If the meat roll is too long, cut into 2 shorter rolls.

3. Create a bowl of aluminum foil that will hold the meat roll or rolls. Put the roll/rolls in the foil bowl and put the foil on top of the potatoes.

4. Cover and lock the lid. Turn the steam valve to "Sealing". Press the "Manual" key, set the pressure to "High", and set the timer to 35 minutes.

5. When the instant pot timer beeps, turn the steam valve to "Venting" to quickly release the pressure. Unlock and carefully open the lid.

6. Remove the foil with the meatloaf.

7. Mash the potatoes. Add 2 tablespoons of butter and ¼ cup of milk. Mash until the potato mix is smooth and creamy. Serve!

Nutrition Facts

Per serving | Calories: 676 | Total Fat: 28.4g | Saturated Fat: 15.2g | Cholesterol: 217mg | Sodium: 749mg | Potassium: 1345mg | Carbohydrates: 45.4g | Fiber: 5.7g | Sugars: 4.7g | Protein: 55.4g | Vitamin A: 17% | Vitamin C: 70% | Calcium: 48% | Iron: 133%

Pina Colada Chicken

Yield: 4 servings

Time taken: 20 minutes

Ingredients

- 2 pounds chicken thighs, organic, cut into 1-inch chunks
- ⅛ teaspoon salt
- ½ cup green onion, chopped, for garnish
- ½ cup coconut cream, full fat
- 1 teaspoon cinnamon
- 1 cup pineapple chunks, frozen or fresh
- 2 tablespoons coconut aminos

Directions

1. Except for the green onions, put the rest of the ingredients in the instant pot.
2. Cover and lock the lid. Turn the steam valve to "Sealing". Press the "Poultry" key and let it cook for 15 minutes preset time.
3. When the instant pot timer beeps, turn off the pot and release the pressure naturally for 10-15 minutes or until the valve drops. Turn the steam valve to "Venting" to release the remaining pressure. Unlock and carefully open the lid.

4. If you want a thick sauce, combine 1 teaspoon arrowroot starch with 1 tablespoon water. Pour the mix in the pot. Press the "Sauté" key and cook until the sauce is thick to your desired form.
5. Turn off the pot. Serve garnished with green onion.

Notes: If you don't have a can of coconut cream, put a can of full-fat coconut milk in the refrigerator and chill overnight. When ready to use, turn the can upside down, open the can and pour out the coconut water that has separated with the coconut cream – you can drink it or save to use for another dish. The coconut cream will be left in the can.

Nutrition Facts

Per serving | Calories: 531 | Total Fat: 24.1g | Saturated Fat: 11g | Cholesterol: 202mg | Sodium: 778mg | Potassium: 731mg | Carbohydrates: 9g | Fiber: 1.9g | Sugars: 5.5g | Protein: 67.7g | Vitamin A: 5% | Vitamin C: 38% | Calcium: 6% | Iron: 21%

Jambalaya

Yield: 5 servings

Time taken: 41 minutes

Ingredients

- 1½ pounds chicken breast, cut into in 1-inch cubes
- 1 can (24 ounces) diced tomatoes (or an equal amount of fresh)
- 1 pound shrimp, wild-caught, uncooked, tails and peels removed, roughly chopped
- 1 tablespoon Cajun seasoning
- 1 tablespoon dried parsley
- 1 teaspoon Cajun seasoning
- 1 teaspoon salt
- 1 yellow onion, medium-sized, diced
- 12 ounces chicken andouille sausage, nitrate free, sliced
- 2 cups sprouted brown rice
- 2 sage leaves, large-sized, bruised and torn
- 2 teaspoons salt
- 3 cloves garlic, minced
- 3 cups bone broth
- 4 tablespoons lard (or other fat of choice), divided

Directions

1. Press the "Sauté" key of the instant pot. Put the lard in the pot and melt. Add the chicken breast and cook until the meat is no longer pink.
2. Add the sausage and stir to combine. Cook for about 3 to 4 minutes. Add the shrimp and season with 1 teaspoon Cajun seasoning and 1 teaspoon salt. Stir to coat and cook until the shrimp is no longer pink. Transfer the chicken mix into a plate.
3. Add the remaining 2 tablespoons of lard into the pot. Add the onion and sauté until soft. Add the garlic and the tomatoes. Add the rice, broth and remaining Cajun seasoning and salt. Stir to combine.
4. Press the "Cancel" key to stop the sauté function. Cover and lock the lid. Turn the steam valve to "Sealing". Press the "Manual" key, set the pressure to "High", and set the timer to 26 minutes.
5. When the instant pot timer beeps, turn the steam valve to "Venting" to quickly release the pressure. Unlock and carefully open the lid.
6. Add the chicken mixture into the pot and stir to combine. Top with the dried parsley. Serve.

Nutrition Facts

Per serving | Calories: 818 | Total Fat: 36.5g | Saturated Fat: 12g | Cholesterol: 280mg | Sodium: 2658mg | Potassium: 1132mg | Carbohydrates: 68.3g | Fiber: 5.1g | Sugars: 5g | Protein: 51.7g | Vitamin A: 31% | Vitamin C: 37% | Calcium: 20% | Iron: 21%

Marinated Steak

Yield: 4 servings

Time taken: 55 minutes

Ingredients

- 2 pounds flank steak
- ¼ cup apple cider vinegar
- ½ cup olive oil
- 1 tablespoon Worcestershire sauce
- 2 tablespoons onion soup mix, dried

Directions

1. Press the "Sauté" key of the instant pot. Add the flank and cook until each side is brown. Add the Worcestershire sauce, vinegar, onion soup mix and the olive oil.
2. Press the "Cancel" key to stop the sauté function. Cover and lock the lid. Turn the steam valve to "Sealing". Press the "Meat/Stew" key, set the pressure to "High", and set the timer to 35 minutes.
3. When the instant pot timer beeps, release the pressure naturally for 5 minutes. Turn the steam valve to "Venting" to release the remaining pressure. Unlock and carefully open the lid. Serve!

Nutrition Facts

Per serving | Calories: 684 | Total Fat: 44.1g | Saturated Fat: 11.4g | Cholesterol: 125mg | Sodium: 738mg | Potassium: 829mg | Carbohydrates: 5.5g | Fiber: 0g | Sugars: 1.1g | Protein: 63.6g | Vitamin A: 0% | Vitamin C: 0% | Calcium: 5% | Iron: 24%

Chicken, Broccoli, and Cheddar Pasta

Yield: 4 servings

Time taken: 9 minutes

Ingredients

- 1 bag (16 ounces) frozen broccoli
- 1 cup milk OR half-and-half
- 1 pound grilled chicken, optional
- 1 pound pasta
- 16 ounces cheddar cheese
- 4 cups water

Directions

1. Put the pasta in the instant pot. Pour the water in the pot. Top with the frozen broccoli.
2. Cover and lock the lid. Turn the steam valve to "Sealing". Press the "Manual" key, set the pressure to "High", and set the timer to 4 minutes.
3. When the instant pot timer beeps, turn the steam valve to "Venting" to quickly release the pressure. Unlock and carefully open the lid. Press the "Sauté" key. Add the cheese and milk in the pot. Stir and mix until the cheese is melted. If using chicken, stir in the chicken. Serve.

Nutrition Facts

Per serving | Calories: 894 | Total Fat: 43.5g | Saturated Fat: 25.5g | Cholesterol: 226mg | Sodium: 826mg | Potassium: 774mg | Carbohydrates: 74g | Fiber: 3g | Sugars: 5.3g | Protein: 52.5g | Vitamin A: 38% | Vitamin C: 169% | Calcium: 100% | Iron: 30%

Wild Rice and Chicken

Yield: 4 servings

Time taken: 55 minutes

Ingredients

- 2 cups chicken breast, uncooked, cut into cubes
- 3½ cups chicken broth
- 1 cup wild rice, long grain
- 2 cups brown rice
- 2 tablespoons butter OR olive oil
- 2 tablespoons soy sauce
- Salt and pepper, to taste
- 1 cup frozen vegetable (mushrooms, carrots, peas, or broccoli)

Directions

1. Pour the chicken broth in the instant pot and press the "Sauté" key – this will heat it up while you prepare the other ingredients.
2. Prepare the chicken and, if using, the vegetables.
3. Add the rest of the ingredients in the pot.
4. Press the "Cancel" key to stop the sauté function. Cover and lock the lid. Turn the steam valve to "Sealing". Press the "Manual" key, set the pressure to "High", and set the timer to 35 minutes.

5. When the instant pot timer beeps, turn the steam valve to "Venting" to quickly release the pressure. Unlock and carefully open the lid. Serve.

Nutrition Facts

Per serving | Calories: 689 | Total Fat: 13.3g | Saturated Fat: 5.5g | Cholesterol: 53mg | Sodium: 1220mg | Potassium: 829mg | Carbohydrates: 109.7g | Fiber: 7.8g | Sugars: 3.2g | Protein: 31.6g | Vitamin A: 43% | Vitamin C: 2% | Calcium: 13% | Iron: 20%

Pork Tenderloin Teriyaki

Yield: 4 servings

Time taken: 40 minutes

Ingredients

- 2 pork tenderloins, cut into half
- 2 green onions, chopped
- 2 cups teriyaki sauce
- 2 tablespoons canola oil OR similar
- Generous pinches salt and pepper
- Toasted sesame seeds

Directions

1. Press the "Sauté" key of the instant pot and put in the oil. When hot, put a pork tenderloin or two in the pot and cook for a couple of minutes or until some of the sides are lightly brown.
2. When the tenderloins are brown, pour the teriyaki sauce over the top of the tenderloins.
3. Press the "Cancel" key to stop the sauté function. Cover and lock the lid. Turn the steam valve to "Sealing". Press the "Manual" key, set the pressure to "High", and set the timer to 20 minutes.
4. When the instant pot timer beeps, release the pressure naturally for 10-15 minutes or until the valve drops. Turn the steam valve to "Venting" to release the remaining pressure. Unlock and carefully open the lid.

5. Slice the meat and serve with steamed broccoli and jasmine rice. Garnish each serving with chopped green onions and toasted sesame seeds.

Nutrition Facts

Per serving | Calories: 306 | Total Fat: 11.6g | Saturated Fat: 2.2g | Cholesterol: 53mg | Sodium: 5557mg | Potassium: 596mg | Carbohydrates: 23g | Fiber: 0g | Sugars: 20.5g | Protein: 25.6g | Vitamin A: 2% | Vitamin C: 3% | Calcium: 4% | Iron: 19%

Meatball Bubble Up

Yield: 2 servings

Time taken: 30 minutes

Ingredients

- 1 bag (1 pound) frozen meatballs
- 8 ounces cheese, your favorite, shredded
- 1 can refrigerated biscuits
- 1 cup water, for the pot
- 1 jar sauce, your favorite
- ¼ cup fresh parsley, chopped
- 4 fresh basil leaves, chopped

Directions

1. In a mixing bowl, mix the meatballs with the cheese, sauce, basil, and parsley; set aside.
2. Cut the biscuits into 4 pieces. Mix the biscuit pieces with the meatball mix.
3. Pour the contents into a spring-form pan or a Pyrex that will fit your instant pot.
4. Pour the water in the pot. Set a trivet in the bottom. Set the spring-form pan or a Pyrex on the trivet.
5. Cover and lock the lid. Turn the steam valve to "Sealing". Press the "Manual" key, set the pressure to "High", and set the timer to 15 minutes.

6. When the instant pot timer beeps, turn the steam valve to "Venting" to quickly release the pressure. Unlock and carefully open the lid. Serve!

Nutrition Facts

Per serving | Calories: 789 | Total Fat: 37.8g | Saturated Fat: 18.7g | Cholesterol: 107mg | Sodium: 3538mg | Potassium: 177mg | Carbohydrates: 72.5g | Fiber: 2.5g | Sugars: 40g | Protein: 38.6g | Vitamin A: 18% | Vitamin C: 8% | Calcium: 43% | Iron: 13%

Pot Roast Ultimate

Yield: 4 servings

Time taken: 45 minutes

Ingredients

- 2-3 pounds chuck roast
- 4 potatoes, large-sized, cut into large cubes
- 4 carrots, chopped
- 3 tablespoons steak sauce, optional
- 3 cloves garlic
- 2 tablespoons olive oil
- 2 tablespoons Italian seasonings
- 2 stalks celery, chopped
- 1 onion
- 1 cup beef broth
- 1 cup red wine

Directions

1. Press the "Sauté" key of the instant pot. Pour in the olive oil. Add the roast and cook each side for about 1-2 minutes or until both sides are brown.
2. Transfer the roast on a plate. Put the carrots, potatoes, and celery in the pot. Top with the garlic and onion. Pour in the beef broth and wine. Put the roast on top of the vegetables. Spread the seasoning over the top of the roast and then spread with the sauce.

3. Press the "Cancel" key to stop the sauté function. Cover and lock the lid. Turn the steam valve to "Sealing". Press the "Manual" key, set the pressure to "High", and set the timer to 35 minutes.
4. When the instant pot timer beeps, release the pressure naturally for 10-15 minutes or until the valve drops. Turn the steam valve to "Venting" to release the remaining pressure. Unlock and carefully open the lid. Serve!

Nutrition Facts

Per serving | Calories: 827 | Total Fat: 28.5g | Saturated Fat: 8.3g | Cholesterol: 234mg | Sodium: 584mg | Potassium: 1902mg | Carbohydrates: 47.5g | Fiber: 7.4g | Sugars: 9.2g | Protein: 80.8g | Vitamin A: 205% | Vitamin C: 81% | Calcium: 8% | Iron: 58%

Chapter 5: Desserts

Pumpkin Chocolate Chip Bundt Cake

Yield: 1 cake

Time taken: 1 hour and 10 minutes

Ingredients

- 1 medium-sized banana, peeled and mashed
- ¾ cup all-purpose flour, unbleached and sifted
- ⅔ cup semi-sweet chocolate chips
- ¾ cup whole-wheat flour, sifted

- ½ teaspoon salt
- ¾ cup white sugar
- ¾ teaspoon pumpkin pie spice
- 1 teaspoon baking soda
- ½ teaspoon vanilla extract
- ½ teaspoon baking powder
- 2 tablespoons canola or avocado oil
- 1 egg
- ½ cup Greek yogurt
- 7.5 ounces pumpkin puree
- 1½ cups water

Directions

1. Place flour in a medium-sized bowl and stir in salt, pumpkin pie spice, baking soda, and baking powder; set aside until required.
2. Crack an egg in a separate large bowl and, using an electric mixer, whisk in mashed banana, vanilla, sugar, oil, yogurt, and pumpkin puree.
3. At slow speed, whisk in flour mixture, 2 tablespoons at a time, until incorporated.
4. Then fold in chocolate chips.
5. Take a Bundt pan, grease the inner sides with a non-stick cooking spray, and spoon in the prepared cake batter.
6. Cover Bundt pan with paper towels and then wrap completely with aluminum foil by first covering the

bottom and then roll the foil edges and combine the edges at the top, forming a handle.

7. Pour water in an instant pot and insert trivet stand.
8. Place Bundt pan on the stand, then plug in instant pot and cover with its lid.
9. Select the "Manual" option and adjust cooking time to 35 minutes.
10. Then choose the high-pressure cooking setting and let cook.
11. The cooking timer will start once the pressure builds, about 10 to 12 minutes.
12. Upon beeping of the timer, press "Cancel" and select the "Keep warm" option, or unplug the instant pot, and let pressure release naturally.
13. When the pressure is released completely, uncover the instant pot, and remove the pan.
14. Let pan cool slightly before uncovering it.
15. Take out the cake, let cool completely on wire rack, and then slice to serve.

Nutrition Facts

Per serving | Calories: 2586 | Total Fat: 80.86g | Saturated Fat: 30.66g | Cholesterol: 181mg | Sodium: 2622mg | Potassium: 2836mg | Carbohydrates: 429.05g | Fiber: 27.7g | Sugars: 251.68g | Protein: 48.67g | Vitamin A: 542% | Vitamin C: 27% | Calcium: 60% | Iron: 128%

Baked Apples

Yield: 6 apples

Time taken: 30 minutes

Ingredients

- 6 medium-sized apples, cored
- 2 tablespoons ground cinnamon
- ½ cup white sugar
- 1 cup apple juice
- Whipped cream for serving

Directions

1. Into an instant pot, place apples and pour in the juice.
2. Evenly sprinkle with sugar and ground cinnamon.
3. Plug in the instant pot, close the lid, and make sure pressure indicator is positioned to its right place.
4. Select the "Manual" option and adjust cooking time to 8 minutes.
5. Then choose the high-pressure cooking setting and let cook.
6. The cooking timer will start once the pressure builds, about 10 to 12 minutes.
7. Upon beeping of the timer, press "Cancel" and select the "Keep warm" option, or unplug the instant pot, and let pressure release naturally.

8. When the pressure is released completely, uncover the instant pot, and transfer apples into serving bowls.
9. Drizzle with cooking liquid and serve with whipped cream.

Nutrition Facts

Per serving | Calories: 190 | Total Fat: 0.44g | Saturated Fat: 0.099g | Cholesterol: 0mg | Sodium: 9mg | Potassium: 272mg | Carbohydrates: 49.91g | Fiber: 5.8g | Sugars: 40.75g | Protein: 0.65g | Vitamin A: 5% | Vitamin C: 33% | Calcium: 6% | Iron: 3%

Thai Coconut Rice

Yield: 4 servings

Time taken: 45 minutes

Ingredients

- 1 large mango, peeled, cored and sliced
- 1 cup Thai sweet rice
- ⅛ teaspoon salt
- 4 teaspoon sugar cane
- ½ teaspoon cornstarch
- Sesame seeds as needed for garnishing
- 1 can (13.5 oz) full fat coconut milk
- 1½ cups water

Directions

1. Place rice in an instant pot and pour in water.
2. Then plug in the instant pot and cover with its lid, making sure pressure indicator is positioned to its right place.
3. Select the "Manual" option and adjust cooking time to 3 minutes.
4. Then choose the high-pressure cooking setting and let cook.
5. The cooking timer will start once the pressure builds, which will take 10 to 12 minutes.

6. Meanwhile, place a small saucepan over medium heat, add milk, and stir in salt and sugar.
7. Let cook until sugar is dissolved completely, stirring frequently.
8. When done, set aside this milk mixture until required.
9. Upon beeping of the timer, press "Cancel" and select the "Keep warm" option, or unplug the instant pot, and let pressure release naturally.
10. When the pressure is released completely, uncover the instant pot, and stir in ½ of the prepared milk mixture.
11. Wrap the instant pot lid with a tea towel, then return the lid to the instant pot and let rest for 5 to 10 minutes.
12. Meanwhile, return saucepan to low heat and heat remaining milk mixture until warm.
13. Stir together cornstarch and 2 tablespoons water and add to the milk mixture.
14. Stir continuously and let cook until mixture is thick and creamy.
15. Transfer rice on a serving platter, top with milk sauce, garnish with sesame seeds, and serve with mango slices.

Nutrition Facts

Per serving | Calories: 369 | Total Fat: 24.95g | Saturated Fat: 20.573g | Cholesterol: 0mg | Sodium: 245mg | Potassium: 425mg | Carbohydrates: 36.99g | Fiber: 4.1g | Sugars: 21.12g | Protein: 4.59g | Vitamin A: 39% | Vitamin C: 44% | Calcium: 7% | Iron: 15%

Egg Custard

Yield: 5 ramekins

Time taken: 30 minutes

Ingredients

- 3 eggs
- 1½ cups unsweetened whole milk, divided
- ⅛ teaspoon salt
- 5 tablespoons white sugar
- 1 cup water

Directions

1. Pour 1 cup milk in an instant pot and stir in sugar and salt until just mixed.
2. Select the "Slow cook" option and let cook until sugar melts completely, stirring frequently.
3. Transfer milk to a bowl and let cool so it is not too hot to touch.
4. Then stir in remaining ½ cup milk until well mixed.
5. Crack eggs in a separate large bowl and whisk until blended.
6. Continue whisking and blend in milk until well mixed.
7. Pass this mixture twice through a fine mesh strainer until ultra-smooth; discard solids collected in the strainer.

8. Evenly divide egg mixture into 4 to 5 ramekins (3 x 1.5 inches).
9. With a spoon, remove bubbles from the top of mixture and tightly wrap each ramekin with aluminum foil.
10. Rinse instant pot, pour in water, and insert trivet stand or steamer basket.
11. Carefully stack covered ramekins on the trivet or basket in two layers.
12. Plug in the instant pot, close the lid, and make sure pressure indicator is positioned to its right place.
13. Select the "Manual" option and adjust cooking time to 0 (zero) minute or 1 (one) minute if aluminum foil is thick.
14. Then choose the low-pressure cooking setting and let cook.
15. The cooking timer will start once the pressure builds, about 10 to 12 minutes.
16. Upon beeping of the timer, press "Cancel" and select the "Keep warm" option, or unplug the instant pot, and let pressure release naturally.
17. When the pressure is released completely, uncover the instant pot, and carefully remove ramekins from the instant pot.
18. Uncover ramekins and serve immediately.

Nutrition Facts

Per serving | Calories: 131 | Total Fat: 4.9g | Saturated Fat: 2.19g | Cholesterol: 106mg | Sodium: 132mg | Potassium: 133mg | Carbohydrates: 16.19g | Fiber: 0g | Sugars: 16.27g |

Protein: 5.62g | Vitamin A: 11% | Vitamin C: 0% | Calcium: 10% | Iron: 3%

Tapioca Pudding

Yield: 2 servings

Time taken: 1 hour and 35 minutes

Ingredients

- ⅓ cup tapioca pearls
- ⅛ teaspoon sea salt
- ¼ teaspoon ground nutmeg
- ¼ cup maple syrup or to taste
- 1 teaspoon vanilla extract
- 13.5 ounces full fat coconut milk
- 1 cup water

Directions

1. Take an oven proof bowl, large enough to fit into the instant pot, and place all the ingredients in it, except for water.
2. Whisk until well combined.
3. Pour water into the instant pot, insert steamer basket or trivet stand, and place bowl on it.
4. Plug in the instant pot, close the lid, and make sure pressure indicator is positioned to its right place.
5. Select the "Manual" option and adjust cooking time to 20 minutes. Then choose the high-pressure cooking setting and let cook.

6. The cooking timer will start once the pressure builds, about 10 to 12 minutes.
7. Upon beeping of the timer, press "Cancel" and select the "Keep warm" option, or unplug the instant pot, and do quick pressure release.
8. When the pressure is released completely, uncover the instant pot, and remove the bowl.
9. Stir until mixed and transfer bowl into the refrigerator and let chill for 1 hour or until cooled and thick.
10. Serve with sliced fruits.

Nutrition Facts

Per serving | Calories: 640 | Total Fat: 45.76g | Saturated Fat: 40.53g | Cholesterol: 0mg | Sodium: 191mg | Potassium: 594mg | Carbohydrates: 59.69g | Fiber: 4.5g | Sugars: 31.33g | Protein: 4.46g | Vitamin A: 0% | Vitamin C: 7% | Calcium: 9% | Iron: 20%

Applesauce

Yield: Makes approximately 3 cups of applesauce.

Time taken: 20 minutes

Ingredients

- 8 medium-sized apples, cored
- 1 teaspoon ground cinnamon
- 1 cup water

Directions

1. Cut apples into 2-inch pieces and place in an instant pot.
2. Pour in water, then plug in the instant pot, close the lid, making sure pressure indicator is positioned to its right place.
3. Select the "Manual" option and adjust cooking time to 8 minutes.
4. Then choose the high-pressure cooking setting and let cook.
5. The cooking timer will start once the pressure builds, about 10 to 12 minutes.
6. Upon beeping of the timer, press "Cancel" and select the "Keep warm" option, or unplug the instant pot, and after 3 minutes, do quick pressure release.
7. When the pressure is released completely, uncover the instant pot, and drain excess cooking liquid.

8. Then, using an immersion blender, blend apples until sauce reaches desired consistency, either smooth or slightly lumpy.
9. Stir in cinnamon and let the sauce cool completely.
10. Store sauce in sterilized dry pint jars and serve when required.

Nutrition Facts

Per serving | Calories: 255 | Total Fat: 0.84g | Saturated Fat: 0.139g | Cholesterol: 0mg | Sodium: 7mg | Potassium: 523mg | Carbohydrates: 67.72g | Fiber: 12.1g | Sugars: 50.44g | Protein: 1.3g | Vitamin A: 11% | Vitamin C: 30% | Calcium: 5% | Iron: 4%

Raspberry Chocolate Chip Mug Cakes

Yield: 1 mug cake

Time taken: 30 minutes

Ingredients

- ½ cup fresh raspberries
- 1½ tablespoons chocolate chips
- ⅓ cup almond flour
- ⅛ teaspoon salt
- 1 tablespoon maple syrup
- ½ teaspoon vanilla extract
- 1 egg

Directions

1. In a bowl, stir together flour and salt until combined.
2. In a separate large bowl, using an electric mixer, whisk together egg, maple syrup, and vanilla until combined.
3. At low speed, whisk in flour mixture until incorporated.
4. Fold in raspberries and chocolate chips.
5. Take 8-ounce mason jars, grease the inner sides with non-stick cooking spray, and spoon in the prepared cake batter, and don't overfill.
6. Pour water in an instant pot and insert trivet stand.
7. Cover jars tightly with aluminum foil and place on the trivet stand.

8. Plug in the instant pot, close the lid, and make sure pressure indicator is positioned to its right place.
9. Select the "Manual" option and adjust cooking time to 10 minutes.
10. Then choose the high-pressure cooking setting and let cook.
11. The cooking timer will start once the pressure builds, about 10 to 12 minutes.
12. Upon beeping of the timer, press "Cancel" and select the "Keep warm" option, or unplug the instant pot, and do quick pressure release.
13. When the pressure is released completely, uncover the instant pot, and carefully transfer jars to a cooling rack with tongs.
14. Uncover jars, let cool slightly for 5 minutes, and serve straightaway.

Nutrition Facts

Per serving | Calories: 753 | Total Fat: 47.59g | Saturated Fat: 12.637g | Cholesterol: 906mg | Sodium: 663mg | Potassium: 847mg | Carbohydrates: 42.59g | Fiber: 9.9g | Sugars: 27.02g | Protein: 39.81g | Vitamin A: 58% | Vitamin C: 21% | Calcium: 28% | Iron: 42%

Raspberry Curd

Yield: 4 servings

Time taken: 25 minutes + cooling time

Ingredients

- 12 ounces raspberries, fresh
- 1 cup white sugar
- 2 tablespoons unsalted butter
- 2 tablespoons lemon juice
- 2 egg yolks

Directions

1. Place raspberries in an instant pot, add lemon juice and sugar, and stir until combined.
2. Plug in the instant pot, close the lid, and make sure pressure indicator is positioned to its right place.
3. Select the "Manual" option and adjust cooking time to 1 minute.
4. Then choose the high-pressure cooking setting and let cook.
5. The cooking timer will start once the pressure builds, about 10 to 12 minutes.
6. Upon beeping of the timer, press "Cancel" and select the "Keep warm" option, or unplug the instant pot, and after 5 minutes, do quick pressure release.
7. Meanwhile, in a bowl, whisk egg yolks until blended.

8. When the pressure is released completely, uncover the instant pot, and immediately pass the mixture through a fine mesh strainer.
9. Remove and discard solids left in the strainer and gradually whisk the collected puree into the egg yolk mixture.
10. Return the mixture to the instant pot, then plug in the instant pot and press the "Sauté" option.
11. Let cook until mixture comes to boiling, stirring constantly.
12. Then switch off the instant pot and stir in butter until mixed.
13. Transfer curd into a container and let cool at room temperature.
14. Place curd in the refrigerator and serve when required.

Nutrition Facts

Per serving | Calories: 302 | Total Fat: 6.68g | Saturated Fat: 3.234g | Cholesterol: 100mg | Sodium: 8mg | Potassium: 152mg | Carbohydrates: 60.98g | Fiber: 5.6g | Sugars: 53.9g | Protein: 2.63g | Vitamin A: 12% | Vitamin C: 34% | Calcium: 4% | Iron: 5%

New York Cheesecake

Yield: 12 servings

Time taken: 55 minutes

Ingredients

- 2 eggs
- 16 ounces cream cheese
- 15 Oreo's
- 1 tablespoon vanilla
- 1 cup sugar
- 2 tablespoons butter, melted

Equipment:

- 7-inch spring-form pan

Directions

1. Put the Oreos into a food processor. Stir in the melted butter. Process until well combined.
2. Press the Oreos mix into the bottom of the spring-form pan.
3. In a medium to large-sized bowl, combine the cream cheese with the eggs, vanilla, and sugar. Mix until the ingredients is creamy and smooth. Scoop the mix into the spring form pan.
4. Set a trivet in the bottom of the instant pot and pour in 1 cup of water in the pot.

5. Place the spring-form pan on the trivet. Cover and lock the lid. Turn the steam valve to "Sealing". Press the "Manual" key, set the pressure to "High", and set the timer to 40 minutes.
6. When the instant pot timer beeps, turn the steam valve to "Venting" to quickly release the pressure. Unlock and carefully open the lid.
7. Chill in the refrigerator for 1 hour and top with fruits or your favorite topping.

Nutrition Facts

Per serving | Calories: 283 | Total Fat: 18.2g | Saturated Fat: 10.2g | Cholesterol: 74mg | Sodium: 196mg | Potassium: 80mg | Carbohydrates: 26.8g | Fiber: 0g | Sugars: 22g | Protein: 4.5g | Vitamin A: 12% | Vitamin C: 0% | Calcium: 4% | Iron: 6%

Apple Bread with Salted Caramel Icing

Yield: 10 servings

Time taken: 20-30 minutes (Preparation Time) + 70 minutes (Cooking Time)

Ingredients

- 3 cups apples, peeled, cored, and cubed
- 2 eggs
- 2 cups flour
- 1 tablespoon vanilla
- 1 tablespoon baking powder
- 1 tablespoon apple pie spice
- 1 stick butter
- 1 cup sugar

For the topping:

- 1 cup heavy cream
- 1 stick salted butter
- 2 cups brown sugar
- 2 cups powdered sugar

Directions

1. Put the eggs, butter, sugar, apple pie spice in the mixer; cream until smooth and creamy. Stir in the apples.

2. In a different bowl, mix the flour with the baking powder. Add the flour mixture into the wet mix, adding half of the flour mixture at a time – the batter will be thick. Pour the mix into the spring-form pan.
3. Set a trivet in the instant pot and pour 1 cup of water in the pot. Place the spring-form pan on the trivet.
4. Cover and lock the lid. Turn the steam valve to "Sealing". Press the "Manual" key, set the pressure to "High", and set the timer to 70 minutes.
5. While the cake is cooking in the pot, prepare the icing. Put the butter in a small-sized saucepan and melt. Add brown sugar and let come to a boil. Continue cooking for 3 minutes or until the sugar is melted. Stir in the heavy cream and continue cooking for about 2 to 3 minutes or until slightly thick. Remove the saucepan from the heat and let it completely cool. Mix in the powdered sugar and whisk until there are no more lumps and creamy.
6. When the instant pot timer beeps, turn the steam valve to "Venting" to quickly release the pressure. Unlock and carefully open the lid.
7. Remove the spring-form pan from the pot and top the apple bread with the icing.

Nutrition Facts

Per serving | Calories: 523 | Total Fat: 20.1g | Saturated Fat: 12.3g | Cholesterol: 81mg | Sodium: 132mg | Potassium: 267mg | Carbohydrates: 85.3g | Fiber: 2g | Sugars: 65.8g |

Protein: 3.6g | Vitamin A: 13% | Vitamin C: 7% | Calcium: 10% | Iron: 10%

Crème Brulee Cheesecake Bites

Yield: 18 servings

Time taken: 40 minutes

Ingredients

For the cheesecake crust:

- 6-8 (about 3.2 ounces) graham crackers, finely ground
- 3-4 tablespoons (about 1.5-2 ounces) unsalted butter, melted
- 2 teaspoons-1½ tablespoons (about 0.3-0.7 ounces) brown sugar (depending on your desired sweetness)
- Sea salt, pinch
- Optional ⅓ cup (about 1.1 ounces) all-purpose flour (for blind baking the crust)

For the cheesecake mixture:

- 16 ounces cream cheese, room temperature
- ½ cup (about 4.2 ounces) sour cream, room temperature
- 2 eggs, large-sized, room temperature
- 2 tablespoons (about 0.6 ounces) cornstarch
- 2 teaspoons vanilla extract
- ⅔ cup (about 4.7 ounces) white sugar
- Sea salt, pinch

For the crackable Caramel:

- 1½-2 teaspoons white sugar, per cheesecake bite

Equipment:

- 18 pieces mini silicone cups

Directions

For the cheesecake crust:

1. Put the graham crackers into a food processor and process until finely ground. Alternatively, you can put the graham crackers in a Ziploc bag and roll with a rolling pin until finely ground. Or, you can buy already finely ground pack.
2. In a small-sized mixing bowl, mix the graham crackers with the brown sugar, and sea salt using a fork. If blind baking, add the flour. Mix in the unsalted butter until the mix sticks together.
3. Put about 1 tablespoon of graham cracker mix into each silicone baking cups. Using a spoon, gently press down to form into an even layer. Put the baking cups in the freezer until ready to use. If you are blind baking, bake the baking cups in a 325F oven for about 12-25 minutes.

For the cheesecake mixture:

1. In a bowl, mix the cornstarch with the white sugar and sea salt.

2. In a medium-sized mixing bowl, beat the cream cheese using a hand mixer on low speed until creamy. Add ½ of the sugar mix and beat using low speed until mixed. Scrape down the hand mixer and the sides of the bowl using a silicone spatula with every addition of a new ingredient.

3. Add the remaining ½ sugar mix and beat using low speed until mixed.

4. Add the sour cream and the vanilla and beat using low speed until mixed.

5. Adding egg at a time, blend the 2 eggs in the cream cheese mixtures using low speed, one at a time – mix well after adding each egg. Try not to over-mix on this step.

6. Scrape down the hand mixer and the sides of the bowl using a silicone spatula a couple of times to make sure everything is completely mixed.

7. Fill the baking cups ⅔ full with the cream cheese mix.

8. Tap the baking cups against the counter a couple of times to let the air bubbles rise to the surface. Using a toothpick, burst the air bubbles. Tap the baking cups a couple more times until no air bubbles rise to the surface.

Cooking the bites:

1. Pour 1 cup of water into the instant pot. Set a trivet in the bottom of the pot – make sure the trivet is not touching the water. Place the silicone cups on the trivet.

2. Cover and lock the lid. Turn the steam valve to "Sealing". Press the "Manual" key, set the pressure to "High", and set the timer to 7 minutes.
3. When the instant pot timer beeps, release the pressure naturally until the valve drops. Turn the steam valve to "Venting" to release the remaining pressure. Unlock and carefully open the lid.
4. Transfer the baking cups into a wire rack. After a couple of minutes, carefully run your thumb against the rim of the baking cups to prevent the cheesecake from sticking to the sides of the cups.
5. Let the cups cool completely on the wire rack, loosely cover with aluminum foil. Refrigerate for at least 4 to 6 hours.
6. Carefully remove the cheesecake bites from the baking cups. Spread about 1½-2 teaspoons white sugar evenly on the top of each bite. With a culinary torch, melt the sugar until caramelized into a hard crispy top.

Nutrition Facts

Per serving | Calories: 180 | Total Fat: 13g | Saturated Fat: 7.8g | Cholesterol: 54mg | Sodium: 150mg | Potassium: 54mg | Carbohydrates: 13.5g | Fiber: 0g | Sugars: 9.7g | Protein: 3.1g | Vitamin A: 9% | Vitamin C: 0% | Calcium: 3% | Iron: 3%

Chocolate Coated Cheesecake Bites

Yield: 16-20 servings

Time taken: 50 minutes

Ingredients

For the cheesecake crust:

- 6-8 (about 3.2 ounces) graham crackers, finely ground
- 3-4 tablespoons (about 1.5-2 ounces) unsalted butter, melted
- 2 teaspoons-1½ tablespoons (about 0.3-0.7 ounces) brown sugar (depending on your desired sweetness)
- Pinch sea salt
- Optional ⅓ cup (about 1.1 ounces) all-purpose flour (for blind baking the crust)

For the cheesecake mixture:

- 16 ounces cream cheese, room temperature
- ½ cup (about 4.2 ounces) sour cream, room temperature
- 2 eggs, large-sized, room temperature
- 2 tablespoons (about 0.6 ounces) cornstarch
- 2 teaspoons vanilla extract
- ⅔ cup (about 4.7 ounces) white sugar
- Pinch sea salt

191

For the chocolate dipping:

- 300-454 grams (about ⅔-1 pound) of your favorite semi-sweet chocolate bits OR mix in some dark chocolate
- 2-3 tablespoons (about 0.9-1.4 ounces) coconut oil*
  Note: 1 tablespoon coconut oil, per 150 grams (about ⅓ pound) chocolate

Directions

For the cheesecake crust:

1. Put the graham crackers into a food processor and process until finely ground. Alternatively, you can put the graham crackers in a Ziploc bag and roll with a rolling pin until finely ground. Or, you can buy already finely ground pack.
2. In a small-sized mixing bowl, mix the graham crackers with the brown sugar, and sea salt using a fork. If blind baking, add the flour. Mix in the unsalted butter until the mix sticks together.
3. Put about 1 tablespoon graham cracker mix into each silicone baking cups. Using a spoon, gently press down to form into an even layer. Put the baking cups in the freezer until ready to use. If you are blind baking, bake the baking cups in a 325F oven for about 12-25 minutes.

For the cheesecake mixture:

1. In a bowl, mix the cornstarch with the white sugar and sea salt.
2. In a medium-sized mixing bowl, beat the cream cheese using a hand mixer on low speed until creamy. Add ½ of the sugar mix and beat using low speed until mixed. Scrape down the hand mixer and the sides of the bowl using a silicone spatula with every addition of a new ingredient.
3. Add the remaining ½ sugar mix and beat using low speed until mixed.
4. Add the sour cream and the vanilla and beat using low speed until mixed.
5. Adding egg at a time, blend the 2 eggs in the cream cheese mixtures using low speed, one at a time – mix well after adding each egg. Try not to overmix on this step.
6. Scrape down the hand mixer and the sides of the bowl using a silicone spatula a couple of times to make sure everything is completely mixed.
7. Fill the baking cups ⅔ full with the cream cheese mix.
8. Tap the baking cups against the counter a couple of times to let the air bubbles rise to the surface. Using a toothpick, burst the air bubbles. Tap the baking cups a couple more times until no air bubbles rise to the surface.

Cooking the bites:

1. Pour 1 cup of water into the instant pot. Set a trivet in the bottom of the pot – make sure the trivet is not touching the water. Place the silicone cups on the trivet.
2. Cover and lock the lid. Turn the steam valve to "Sealing". Press the "Manual" key, set the pressure to "High", and set the timer to 7 minutes.
3. When the instant pot timer beeps, release the pressure naturally until the valve drops. Turn the steam valve to "Venting" to release the remaining pressure. Unlock and carefully open the lid.
4. Transfer the baking cups into a wire rack. After a couple of minutes, carefully run your thumb against the rim of the baking cups to prevent the cheesecake from sticking to the sides of the cups.
5. Let the cups cool completely on the wire rack, loosely cover with aluminum foil. Refrigerate for at least 4 to 6 hours.

For the chocolate dipping:

1. Fill a saucepan half full with water and bring the water to a boil over high heat. Put the chocolate bits and coconut oil in a mixing bowl that will fit the saucepan. Reduce the heat to gentle heat, stir the chocolate mix until the melted and mixed with the coconut oil.
2. Carefully remove the cheesecake bites from the baking cups. Dip the cheesecake bites into the melted chocolate. Smooth the surface with a fork and place them on a baking tray lined with parchment paper. Put in the freezer for 15 minutes to set the chocolate – do

not leave them long in the freezer or the cheesecake bites will be frozen. Serve immediately.

Nutrition Facts

Per serving | Calories: 317 | Total Fat: 27g | Saturated Fat: 17.1g | Cholesterol: 61mg | Sodium: 178mg | Potassium: 216mg | Carbohydrates: 20.4g | Fiber: 3.3g | Sugars: 10.7g | Protein: 5.9g | Vitamin A: 10% | Vitamin C: 0% | Calcium: 6% | Iron: 22%

Rice Pudding

Yield: 6 servings

Time taken: 30 minutes

Ingredients

- 1 cup basmati rice
- ¾ cup heavy cream OR coconut cream
- 2 cups milk, your choice (soaked nut milk or raw milk)
- ⅛ teaspoon sea salt
- ¼ cup maple syrup
- 1 vanilla bean scrapings OR 1 teaspoon vanilla extract
- 1¼ cups water

Directions

1. Put the rice in a fine mesh colander. Rinse the rice well with several changes of water. Put the washed rice in the instant pot.
2. Add the milk, water, sea salt, and maple syrup in the pot. Stir briefly.
3. Cover and lock the lid. Turn the steam valve to "Sealing". Press the "Porridge" key and let it cook for 20 minutes preset time.
4. When the instant pot timer beeps, release the pressure naturally for 10-15 minutes or until the valve drops. Press the "Cancel" key to stop the keep warm mode.

Turn the steam valve to "Venting" to release the remaining pressure. Unlock and carefully open the lid.

5. Add the vanilla and the cream. Stir well until mixed. Serve with your favorite pudding toppings – berry jam, cream, dates, raisins, nuts, cinnamon, maple syrup, and butter.

Nutrition Facts

Per serving | Calories: 241 | Total Fat: 7.5g | Saturated Fat: 4.5g | Cholesterol: 27mg | Sodium: 87mg | Potassium: 122mg | Carbohydrates: 38g | Fiber: 0g | Sugars: 11.6g | Protein: 5.2g | Vitamin A: 5% | Vitamin C: 0% | Calcium: 13% | Iron: 2%

Pumpkin Pudding

Yield: 5 servings

Time taken: 50 minutes

Ingredients

For the pumpkin pudding:

- ¾ cup pumpkin, packed OR pumpkin puree, homemade, well-drained
- 2 teaspoons gelatin, sustainably-sourced
- ¼ teaspoon ground cloves
- ½ teaspoon sea salt
- ½ teaspoon ground nutmeg
- ½ teaspoon ground ginger
- ½ teaspoon allspice
- ½ cup coconut sugar
- ½ cup coconut milk (raw milk)
- 1 teaspoon ground cinnamon
- 1 egg, pastured
- 1 cup water

For the coconut-ginger glaze:

- 1 teaspoon ground ginger
- Pinch of stevia

- ¾ cup coconut cream, at room temperature

Directions

1. Put the milk into a saucepan. Sprinkle with the gelatin. Turn on the stovetop to medium-low heat to heat the milk gently. Whisk the milk to dissolve the gelatin and then remove from the heat.
2. Pour the milk mixture into a medium-sized mixing bowl. Add the pumpkin, spices, salt, coconut sugar, and egg; whisk until smooth. Pour the mixture into a well-greases 3-cup bowl, jello mold, or soufflé dish.
3. Pour 1 cup water into the instant pot and set a trivet in the bottom of the pot. Place the bowl/mold/dish on the trivet.
4. Cover and lock the lid. Turn the steam valve to "Sealing". Press the "Manual" key, set the pressure to "High", and set the timer to 30 minutes.
5. When the instant pot timer beeps, press the "Cancel" key to stop the keep warm mode and turn the steam valve to "Venting" to quickly release the pressure. Unlock and carefully open the lid.
6. Carefully remove the bowl/mold/dish and let cool to room temperature – do not disturb while it cools. When the pudding is cool, refrigerate for 4-6 hours or until completely set.
7. Run a butter knife around the edge of the pudding and turn over onto a cake stand or a plate.

8. In a small-sized mixing bowl, combine all of the glaze ingredients, whisking until completely smooth. Drizzle the glaze over the finished pudding.
9. If desired, garnish with crispy walnuts and serve.

Notes: You can use any dish that will fit in your instant pot to serve as the mold for the pudding – just grease it will so the pudding will slide out.

Nutrition Facts

Per serving | Calories: 181 | Total Fat: 15.4g | Saturated Fat: 13.1g | Cholesterol: 33mg | Sodium: 217mg | Potassium: 289mg | Carbohydrates: 13.7g | Fiber: 5.2g | Sugars: 4.5g | Protein: 4.7g | Vitamin A: 115% | Vitamin C: 6% | Calcium: 4% | Iron: 11%

Apple Crisp

Yield: 8 servings

Time taken: 18 minutes

Ingredients

- 5-6 apples, medium-sized (I used Fuji, your preferred variety)
- 2 teaspoons ground cinnamon
- ½ cup water
- ½ cup flour blend (I used Bob's Red Mill 1:1 Gluten Free)
- ½ cup butter, melted
- ½ cup brown sugar, organic
- 1 cup oats, gluten free

Directions

1. Peel the apples and remove the seeds. Slice into thin pieces and put the slices in the bottom of the instant pot.
2. Stir the cinnamon in the water and pour over the apples in the pot.
3. Stir the remaining ingredients together until well combined and spread the mix over the top of the apple mix in the pot.

4. Cover and lock the lid. Turn the steam valve to "Sealing". Press the "Manual" key, set the pressure to "High", and set the timer to 8 minutes.
5. When the instant pot timer beeps, press the "Cancel" key to stop the keep warm mode and release the pressure naturally for 10 minutes. Turn the steam valve to "Venting" to release the remaining pressure. Unlock and carefully open the lid.
6. Let the apple crisp cool for a bit. Serve!

Notes: If you want more crumble topping, double the oats, butter, flour, and brown sugar mix. Likewise, if you are using Granny Smith or tart apple, add more maple syrup to sweeten them a bit.

Nutrition Facts

Per serving | Calories: 277 | Total Fat: 12.5g | Saturated Fat: 7.4g | Cholesterol: 31mg | Sodium: 87mg | Potassium: 213mg | Carbohydrates: 41.5g | Fiber: 4.9g | Sugars: 23.4g | Protein: 2.7g | Vitamin A: 7% | Vitamin C: 18% | Calcium: 2% | Iron: 8%

Stuffed Peaches

Yield: 5 servings

Time taken: 8 minutes

Ingredients

- 5 peaches, medium-sized, organic OR 6 small-sized peaches
- 2 tablespoons butter, grass-fed
- ¼ teaspoon pure almond extract
- ¼ cup maple sugar OR mascobado OR sucanat
- ¼ cup cassava flour (I used Otto's)
- ½ teaspoon ground cinnamon
- Pinch Celtic sea salt

For the Instant Pot

- ¼ teaspoon pure almond extract
- 1 cup water

Directions

1. Slice ¼-inch off from the tops of the peaches. With a sharp paring knife, cut around the center of the peaches and remove the pits to hollow out the peaches – leave at least ½-inch of the flesh so that the peaches stay intact. If the peaches are very firm, use a spoon to

203

help loosen and scoop out the pit and the flesh around the pit. Set the hollowed peaches aside.

2. In a shallow dish or a mixing bowl, put in the cassava flour. Add the sweetener, cinnamon, sea salt, butter, and almond extract. Using clean hands, mix together until the mixture is crumbly.

3. Fill the hollowed out peaches with the crumble mixture until filled to the top.

4. Pour water into the instant pot and add ¼ teaspoon almond extract. Set a steamer basket or steamer insert in the pot. Carefully put the stuffed peaches in the steamer basket/insert.

5. Cover and lock the lid. Turn the steam valve to "Sealing". Press the "Manual" key, set the pressure to "High", and set the timer to 3 minutes.

6. When the instant pot timer beeps, press the "Cancel" key to stop the keep warm mode and turn the steam valve to "Venting" to quickly release the pressure. Unlock and carefully open the lid.

7. Using an oven mitt and tongs, carefully lift and remove the steamer basket/insert and put it in a dish. Let the stuffed peaches rest and cool for about 10 minutes.

8. Serve with vanilla ice cream.

Notes: Use ripe, but still firm peaches – do not use overripe fruits.

Nutrition Facts

Per serving | Calories: 130 | Total Fat: 5g | Saturated Fat: 2.9g | Cholesterol: 12mg | Sodium: 82mg | Potassium: 335mg | Carbohydrates: 21.6g | Fiber: 2.5g | Sugars: 20.1g | Protein: 1.7g | Vitamin A: 12% | Vitamin C: 16% | Calcium: 1% | Iron: 4%

Bread Pudding

Yield: 10-12 servings

Time taken: 40 minutes

Ingredients

- 1 loaf sourdough bread, grain-free, gluten-free
- 1 tablespoon real vanilla extract
- ½ cup butter OR preferred traditional fat, melted
- ½ cup pure maple syrup OR raw honey OR your preferred unrefined sweetener
- ¼ teaspoon sea salt
- 2 cups milk, preferably high-fat coconut or raw
- 2 egg yolks
- 4 eggs

Directions

1. Slice and cut the bread into 1-inch cubes. Select a bowl that will fit in your instant pot, use a metal bowl that is 7½-inch wide and 4-inch high. Put a parchment paper in the bowl, pressing any folds to flatten. Add the cubes into the prepared bowl.
2. Put the eggs, egg yolks, milk, vanilla, maple syrup, and sea salt into a blender. Blend for about 10 to 15 seconds. With the motor of the blender still running,

add the melted butter through the opening in the blender lid. Blend until smooth.

3. Pour the custard mix into the bowl with the bread, pressing on bread gently to wet all cubes. Put a small, square shaped parchment paper over the surface of the pudding – fold any corners from the bottom piece of the parchment paper that may be sticking out.
4. Pour 2 cups of water into the instant pot and set a trivet in the pot. Place the bowl with the bread cubes on the trivet.
5. Cover and lock the lid. Turn the steam valve to "Sealing". Press the "Steam" key and set the timer to 15 minutes.
6. When the instant pot timer beeps, release the pressure naturally for 10-15 minutes or until the valve drops. Turn the steam valve to "Venting" to release the remaining pressure. Press "Cancel" to stop the keep warm mode. Unlock and carefully open the lid.
7. Let the bowl cool slightly and then remove the pudding by lifting up the corners of the parchment paper that line the bowl. Transfer onto a plate and flip over to another plate so the bottom is on the top.
8. Slice and serve, if desired, with caramelized pears. Whipped cream is also a great accompaniment.

Nutrition Facts

Per serving | Calories: 365 | Total Fat: 23.9g | Saturated Fat: 17g | Cholesterol: 132mg | Sodium: 355mg | Potassium: 231mg | Carbohydrates: 31.7g | Fiber: 1.8g | Sugars: 12.1g |

Protein: 7.7g | Vitamin A: 8% | Vitamin C: 2% | Calcium: 5% | Iron: 14%

If you enjoyed this book or received value from it in any way, then I'd like to ask you for a favor: would you be kind enough to leave a review for this book on Amazon? It'd be greatly appreciated!

https://www.amazon.com/dp/1981539549/

Other books by Stephanie N. Collins You can find here

http://dexlerbooks.com/stephanie-n-collins

Made in the USA
Middletown, DE
28 September 2023

39684820R00119